CONNECTED
COLLEAGUES ON PURPOSE

BY YVONNE E. BROOKS
& JOHN W. STANKO

urbanpress

Connected: Colleagues on Purpose
by Yvonne E. Brooks & John W. Stanko
Copyright © 2019 Yvonne E. Brooks & John W. Stanko

ISBN # 978-1-63360-124-6

For Worldwide Distribution Printed in the U.S.A.

Urban Press
P.O. Box 8881
Pittsburgh, PA 15221-0881 USA
412.646.2780

www.urbanpress.us

INTRODUCTION
YVONNE E. BROOKS

In December of 2018, I traveled from the U.K. to Zimbabwe, and as usual, I stopped in South Africa to visit with my friends there. We have three Esther Academy chapters operating in South Africa, and during that time of the year, I usually check to see if they have what they need: journals, registration packs, and the plans for next year's graduation so I can get the dates in my diary.

The 2019 plans were a bit extra special because in August of 2019, I was taking a group of ladies with me. We stopped off in South Africa and then traveled up to Zimbabwe. The plan was to attend the New Life Covenant Church Conference, but due to economic conditions in the country, the conference was cancelled. We still enjoyed the church services that were held and then took some time to go on a safari. We became tourists on our return to South Africa and visited Nelson Mandela's House, saw the Apartheid Museum, and went to some of South Africa's shopping centres because the ladies in the U.K. had no idea what South Africa was like, including their fantastic shopping malls. While we were there, we participated in the graduation for the Esther's Academy 2019 class and a one-day conference called *Next Step*, which is something we also hold in the U.K. This helps the ladies continue the trajectory of their journey into a life that will be played out on the world stage.

I traveled to Zimbabwe in December 2018 because that's the time of year the ladies graduate from the Esther Academy there. They conduct their program slightly differently than we do in the U.K. where we run our program for eight weeks, but they run theirs for eight months. They had 88 ladies graduate in 2018. On one Sunday afternoon, all 88 ladies, dressed in their beautiful ball gowns and some wearing tiaras, came to celebrate the completion of a program I started many years ago for the women in my church in Birmingham, England.

I watched their confidence, deportment, and everything positive about them as they participated in their ceremony. Each lady actually walked a red carpet as she came up to receive her certificate from Bishop Tudor Bismark and me, and then we posed for photographs. After that, we took group photos, which included the 20 or so trainers who had delivered the training throughout the year. It is the high point of my year to go in December for the graduation.

All this may not seem very special for you, but it is for me because I know where I have come from to stand where I am today. I know the difference knowing my purpose has made in my life, for it caused me to sidestep fear and move beyond a lack of resources. I will always be grateful to the Lord and to Dr. John Stanko for helping me discover and live out my purpose. Since I connected with Dr. Stanko and my purpose, I have had one exciting opportunity after another, and that is why I am collaborating on this book with him.

We want to share with you the power of our purpose connection that is available to you just like it was to us. He will tell his story and I will tell mine, and sometimes we will tell our story, in part to give God glory but also to encourage you to connect with your own life purpose—and people who are also purpose seekers.

The 2018 event was our fifth graduation in Zimbabwe, after starting the program there in 2012. They start their program in February and run it for the entire year. We re-started again in 2008 in the U.K., and it's been running ever since. I founded the U.K. Esther Academy in 2001, but when I realized the amount of input that was needed, I actually hit the pause button after the first program so I could have time to assemble a team of the right people.

As I mentioned, the U.K. program runs for eight weeks of actual training, and one of those weeks is a counselling-led segment. If anything emerges for any of the ladies and they recognize their need for God to do something deeper in their heart, they can schedule a one-to-one session with a counselor. Two weeks after the program is completed, we have the graduation banquet, and we make that a big deal. In the U.K., we encourage all the ladies who are graduating (and we keep our classes deliberately small at about 25 ladies) to bring their husbands, fathers, uncles, or another male companion who can escort them into the banqueting hall. Each graduate normally fills up a whole table with family members, so the events are always well attended. We also have entertainment and a keynote speaker or a comedian, and we enjoy a three-course meal. There is a raffle for prizes donated from businesses.

I named this effort The Esther Academy because the Lord had been speaking to me about the woman and queen who has a book of Bible named after her. God wanted the ladies I worked with to be refined, confident, and feminine, but also to be strong. I thought Esther was the perfect example of that in the Bible. When I studied her story, it only confirmed that she was the ideal role model because Esther came out of nowhere and was an orphan raised by a cousin named Mordecai who looked after her day-to-day needs. Mordecai entered her into a royal beauty pageant because the king was looking for a new wife to replace the queen he had deposed.

Because Esther was among the finalists, she resided in the royal palace for an entire year where she was pampered during that time with oils, perfumes, and special beauty treatments. She had to have her hair, wardrobe, deportment, and makeup perfected. Therefore, she is a role model for us, not only because of her beauty, but because when the time came for her to take a stand, she was able to do so with courage and grace. She went from being a ceremonial figurehead to a politician, legislator, and intercessor on behalf of her people. She modeled everything I was looking for in the modern spiritual woman, who could take her place on the world's stage in order to make a stand for her God and her people.

I want to tell you my encounter with the message of purpose and how it changed my life and ministry. If I am going to do that, I have to do it now, for I am 62 years old as I write. What's more, I believe the Lord has shown me He is going to open more doors for my work, and I will need to leave behind a book to help people better understand what I am teaching and the power it has to impact and direct their lives.

It is important at this stage in my life to capture the

information and insight God has given me by writing it down. If I don't have a chance to tell someone while I am alive, this book will be here after I am gone, and people can read it and learn that I was not an overnight success. It has taken me years of experience to get to where I am today and where I will eventually be.

I hope you are impacted with the simplicity of my life. If God used me, He can (and will) use anyone and everyone. I did not have a great start or come from a family with a lot of money. In fact, I was born in Ocho Rios, Jamaica in the West Indies. When my parents migrated to the U.K., we children moved out into the country to stay with my grandmother who agreed to look after us. There we were in a two-room home with one of those pit toilets located a couple hundred yards from the house. There was no electricity, lighting, or any modern facilities or conveniences, including running water. The only running water we had was running off the roof and into our room. That certainly did not set the stage for somebody who would end up being a world-changer.

I am not trying to blow my own trumpet, but when I look back to where I was and what I could have been, based on some of my friends who are still in that situation, and see what God has done, it is cause for both humility and praise for God. I marvel when I see how He orchestrated my life and changed its narrative for me to achieve what He Himself set out to do before the foundation of the world.

I am in awe when I think that my simple message and story of my life will resonate with other women who feel disadvantaged or who did not have opportunities that would have catapulted them onto a world stage of greatness. Even though I had none of those advantages, God still used me, and He is about to do more—and this book is a part of it.

Dr. Stanko and I are going to take turns telling

you our purpose stories and teaching you along the way. We hope to make you laugh (or at least smile) and cause you to think, reflect, and seek your own purpose. You will see from our stories that purpose is now front and center in our minds and hearts, and that won't change any time soon. I pray that you will be able to connect with us and our stories, and that they will help you connect with your own purpose, so let's get started with *Connected: Colleagues on Purpose.*

Pastor Yvonne E. Brooks
Birmingham, U.K.
October 2019

INTRODUCTION
JOHN W. STANKO

In 2001, I made a significant, and what eventually proved to be a traumatic life transition. I left a church I had been with for many years and launched out on my own to start what at first was named the Gold Mine Development Corporation (GMDC). No, it was not a mining entity (although I received many emails promoting mining and metallurgy technology). The company was named after my first book, *Life is a Gold Mine: Can You Dig It?* That book focused on what I called the five Gold Mine Principles, which were designed to help people get their resources "out of the ground of their hearts and minds and into their lives."

I had begun teaching and writing about those gold mine principles—purpose, goals, time management, organization, and faith—in 1985. As I became better known for those principles, over the years invitations came to teach them in various church settings, one of which was in the U.K. There I met a woman named Yvonne Brooks, who enthusiastically received what I taught, especially on the topics of purpose and personality. She took a battery of profiles, one of which was the DISC, and after her session, declared that I *must* come to the church she and her husband pastored in Birmingham, U.K.

When Yvonne invited me, I had more than 20 years of church work under my belt. I was accustomed to people saying things and not following up, so when Pastor Yvonne said, "You must come. I will follow up with an invitation," I politely said, "That would be great," but didn't think much of it. Often people said something like that to be polite, and some I'm sure were sincere but never followed through.

Lo and behold, a few weeks later, I received a call from one Yvonne Brooks following up on her declaration that I needed to visit her church. We set a date for March of 2001, if I remember correctly, and that just happened to coincide with my departure from the church mentioned earlier. I can honestly say, therefore, that visiting New Jerusalem Apostolic Church was my first official visit after I formed GMDC (the church went by a different name at that time).

All I can say is that Yvonne and I connected from the start. She was as enthusiastic then when I first met her (perhaps more so, if that's possible) and she invited a host of people in the church and friends outside the church to meet with me and listen to what I had to say. Such excitement and openness were both flattering and encouraging, and that first visit led to another and then another and another. Before I knew it, Birmingham was a regular stop on my purpose travels.

After a few visits, Pastor Yvonne informed me that she had an organization called Women In the Word, but she was going to rename it Women of Purpose. Again, I was amazed both at this woman's enthusiasm for all things called purpose, and also for her rare ability (at least in my experience) of following up on what she promised to do. With the name change, she felt it appropriate to invite me to the first annual conference under the new name, and I became the best-looking man present at that event (all right, I was the *only* man there, but that still meant I was the most handsome).

At the conference, I spoke and administered the personality profiles, usually holding a one-on-one session with each person to help explain the results. Since some women came from churches other than New Jerusalem, I received invitations to visit those churches, so the purpose message spread and grew throughout the U.K.—thanks to the connection with my friend, Yvonne.

Those early conferences were held during Easter week and I would often stay over for Easter Sunday to speak at a church after attending the New Jerusalem Church Good Friday service. One year, I brought a group of women with me from my college to the conference, and they had an experience they still talk about today. Another Easter Sunday I ended up in London to speak at a Nigerian church in the Hackney, East-London area. For some reason, the church did not invite me out to dinner after I spoke, so I went back to the hotel (which had no restaurant) and found an open Kentucky Fried Chicken, and their three-piece chicken dinner became my Easter feast.

I share that Easter story not to complain but to tell you how much joy I had on that Easter Sunday. I could have not eaten at all, but I would have said like Jesus did, "I have food to eat that you know nothing about" (John 4:32). When I talk, write, counsel, or even think about purpose, I am energized. I remember watching a movie on that Easter Sunday and I saw something that spoke to me of purpose. I told the Lord, "If you want me to spend every Easter Sunday like this, as long as I get to do something on purpose, I will gladly do it!" My connection with the purpose message enhanced my connection with the Lord and brought me many new connections with wonderful purpose seekers like Yvonne. We truly were colleagues on purpose!

When I first began teaching on purpose in 1991, I knew I was on to something special. My first purpose workshop was at an Integrity Music worship weekend in Pismo Beach, California. I was convinced that no one was going to attend my workshop because, after all, this was a worship conference. Who would want to listen to me talk about "Effectiveness: Finding Your Life Purpose"? People did come, however, and during the session, the atmosphere was both sober and electric, if that makes any sense, as people connected with the message.

People actually cried when I spoke about finding purpose. I had caused many people to cry in ministry up to that point, but seldom for the right reasons! This, however, was different. They were weeping because the connection with the message touched something deep in their hearts. People mobbed me after the session and we decided to offer the workshop two months later in Dallas, Texas. The results were the same, and then we moved on to Cincinnati, Florida, Atlanta, and Memphis. After that, the seminar went international and I had a chance to test the purpose message with a non-American audience. Was the purpose message an Americanized topic, or would it "translate" into other cultures? Again, I had my doubts, but we found that it did. I delivered the message in Taiwan, Hong Kong, Australia, New Zealand, and Europe. People couldn't get enough of the message, and I was only too happy to oblige.

Yet there was a problem (a fly in the ointment, as an old saying goes), however, and to me it was a big one. People would cry, laugh, and give me compliments on the message, but when I would ask them, "What do you think your purpose is?", they would often reply, "I have no idea, but the message was so good!" My thought was, *How good can it be if you don't find your purpose?* That caused me to develop probing questions ("What would you do if you had all the money you needed to live on? What do people give you compliments for that you don't think is very special?"), follow-up articles and essays, additional seminars, and eventually books. I then incorporated the personality profiles into my one-on-one coaching sessions (I found I had to make myself available to schedule those after I taught) and that proved to be valuable as a tool to help people, especially Christians, talk about who they are and are not.

When I arrived in Birmingham in 2001, I had 10 years of experience helping people discover their purpose. I was a "bad purpose dude" (an outdated way to say I was good at what I did) who was getting more confident with each passing year. My connection with Pastor Yvonne was a divine appointment and that led us to many exciting experiences and new insights as we worked, talked, counseled, coached, and ministered together. It was a heavenly connection.

Then it all ended—until this book.

I mentioned my church transition at the beginning of this chapter, and eventually the fallout from that transition impacted my relationship with Yvonne. No, we were not angry with each other, but my presence was problematic for her new church affiliations, and I willingly, although sadly, withdrew from the scene. We stayed connected—she still read my weekly *Monday Memo* and I followed her on social media. We would send an occasional message, but my visits and conference participation stopped.

While those things were on a temporary hold, our mutual interest in purpose was not and both of us continued to grow and learn so we could become even more effective at what God had given us to do. It was just a matter of time before we would be reunited, and now here we are, collaborating on a book and ministering together on purpose. It's like we were never apart.

In this book, Pastor Yvonne shares her purpose journey, going back to her childhood. I chose not to go back that far (I am older than Yvonne, and any recollections that far back would be ancient history), but decided to start with 1991, touch on 2001, and then bring you into the present. During that time, I changed the name of my company from Gold Mine Development Company to PurposeQuest Inc., which is the reason I will reference the concept of a purpose quest (sometimes one word) as I go.

Pastor Yvonne will share what she learned about herself and how the purpose message has set her free—and is still doing so. I am going to share my purpose insights so you understand how and why Pastor Yvonne and I connected around the purpose message. We are convinced that the best of our relationship is yet to come, and that's good news for purpose seekers everywhere.

This book is titled *Connected: Colleagues on Purpose* and we hope it inspires, encourages, enlightens, and informs you. If not, we hope that it at least entertains you, for both of us are known to make people laugh—and we love doing that. Along the way, we want to help you connect with us and with the concept we love that changed our lives. We know as you connect with the purpose message, it will change your life as it did ours.

Dr. John W. Stanko
Pittsburgh, PA USA
October 2019

CHAPTER ONE
MY PURPOSE JOURNEY
JOHN W. STANKO

Malcolm Gladwell in his book *Outliers* expressed the belief that when someone devotes 10,000 hours of concentrated study or effort in an area or discipline, that person will be an expert or top performer in his or her field. Author Seth Godin urges his readers to find something they do and perfect it to become one of the best in the world, and then to give their lives to express and perfect it. We will not debate whether the strategies of these two men are valid. I will tell you, however, that I decided to take both men at their word, and I have invested more than 10,000 hours in helping others find purpose because I wanted to be one of the best, most skilled, and anointed purpose coaches in the world. I will leave the results and the "standings" of where I rank in God's hands, but I have paid the price to be the best I can be—and I have no regrets.

The last twenty-five years have been the most fulfilling of my life as I have traveled to 40 countries to address audiences large and small about purpose. Along the way, I have connected through one-on-one purpose sessions with thousands of people. I have focused on my own purpose and saw my understanding of it change ever so slightly, but the change released an avalanche of creativity in me that has yet to cease. I've seen many come to a better understanding of who they are and why they're here as they read what I wrote and listen to what I teach.

We (Yvonne and I) seldom have anyone challenge us as to the validity, worth, or biblical correctness of our purpose presentations. Most everyone intuitively knows the truth about purpose. People familiar with the Bible have at one time or another quoted to someone the words of Romans 8:28: "All things work together for good for those who love God and are called according to His **purpose**" (emphasis added). Perhaps they even know Proverbs 16:4, "The Lord has made everything for its own **purpose**, even the wicked for the day of evil" (NASB, emphasis added).

Many have found that talking about purpose, however, is a lot easier than defining it for themselves in a personal way. Yvonne and I want to help you get beyond *agreeing* that you have a purpose to the point where you can *clearly state the reason* you were born. We're more convinced than ever before that it's possible for everyone to do that, even you. If Yvonne and I did it, so can you.

In our travels and study, we've met many wonderful people who have the same burden we do: to see people doing not just good things, but the best things they were created to do. We've also found that other groups with differing worldview perspectives have pursued this topic and have produced interesting books and articles, some before we ever became colleagues on purpose. For instance, Laurence G. Boldt wrote these words in his book,

How to Find the Work You Love:

> The quest for the work you love—it all begins with the two simple questions: Who am I? And What in the world am I doing here? While as old as humanity itself, these perennial questions are born anew in every man and woman who is privileged to walk upon this earth. Every sane man and woman, at some point in his or her life, is confronted by these questions—some while but children; more in adolescence and youth; still more at mid-life or when facing retirement; and even the toughest customers at the death of a loved one or when they themselves have a brush with death. Yes, somewhere, sometime, we all find ourselves face to face with the questions, Who am I? and What am I here for?
>
> And we do make some attempt to answer them. We ask our parents and teachers, and it seems they do not know. They refer us to political and religious institutions, which often crank out canned answers devoid of personal meaning. Some even tell us that life has no meaning, save for eating and breeding. Most of us are smart enough to recognize that canned answers or begging the question will not do. We must find real answers for ourselves. But that takes more heart and effort than we are often willing to give (Laurence Boldt, *How to Find the Work You Love*. New York: Penguin Books; 1996; page 1).

We agree with much of what Mr. Boldt wrote. We can confirm from our experience that almost everyone faces the issue of purpose at one time or another. You are seeking purpose, or you would not be reading this book or trying to answer the questions: *Who am I? and What am I here for?* People begin their quest for answers at different stages of life, some in childhood and some at retirement. Yvonne and I want to help you find answers to those questions regardless of when you start your search.

Furthermore, religious institutions (i.e. the Church, of which we are both well acquainted) sometimes offer "canned answers" that leave people with simplistic solutions to their purpose questions: *How can I know God's will for my life? How then can I do it?* Often people tell me that they are here "to do the will of God," "to glorify God," "to serve others," or "to worship Him." The problem is that these answers fall short, for you must go further to find the *specific* will of God for your life, *what it is* that will glorify God, *how* you can serve others, and *what it means* to worship God beyond singing a hymn or chorus on Sunday morning.

Since Yvonne and I connected to become friends and colleagues in the purpose vineyard, we have witnessed the release of the best-selling book in the history of publishing (next to the Bible), Rick Warren's *The Purpose-Driven Life*. Despite Pastor Warren's impact, we still find that people are searching and digging for purpose more frantically than ever. In a sense, as purpose possibilities have expanded exponentially, it has created another purpose question in people's minds: *With so many options for what I **can** do, how do I know what I **should** do?*

The pursuit of answers often "takes more heart and effort than we are often willing to give," as Mr. Boldt wrote. It's so much easier to settle for pat answers or to have someone else define who we are, but that's like putting a band-aid on a major laceration. It may look good and even cover the wound, but it won't necessarily bring the desired long-term results, clarity, or fulfillment.

It is common for those who discuss the topic of

purpose to at some point refer to the issue as a life's calling or vocation. The word *vocation* comes from the Latin word *vocare*, which means *to call*. Originally a person could be called or have the vocation of a shoe-maker. Eventually a vocation or call became associated with a religious calling to the priesthood or some other form of ministry. The very concept of a calling means that there is some intelligent force calling the called. A calling comes from someone—God—to someone—His creation.

It is when we seek to serve God and cooperate with His plan that our lives have meaning and direction. As the psalmist wrote, "My help comes from the Lord, the maker of heaven and earth" (Psalm 121:2). The designer of a thing is the perfect one to define the purpose of the item designed, and that is why we look to, even expect, the God of heaven and earth to answer our purpose questions—and He will do the same for you. Mr. Boldt writes,

> Finding the work you love is not a cerebral process. It is not a matter of figuring something out through a process of rational analysis. It is a process of opening yourself and beginning to pay attention to what you respond to with energy and enthusiasm. Pay attention to the people, events, and activities in the outside world that evoke the strongest response from you. Pay attention as well to your inside world, to the inspirations and intuitions that most excite you. From within and without, let yourself be moved. Listen to your own heart and learn to trust what it is saying (Laurence Boldt, *How to Find the Work You Love*. New York: Penguin Books; 1996; page 20).

Our desire is to help you listen and be equipped to see yourself not as others see you, but as God sees you. We encourage you to record your thoughts or impressions as you read, or jot down in your journal other Bible passages you want to look up later. As you set your mind and heart to seek your purpose, it's important to pay attention to your thoughts and impressions that are calling out to you. They may not even make sense when you "hear" them, but it's important that you "honor" them as they come.

Despite the explosion of purpose material, coaches, seminars, books, and movies, people are still asking the questions mentioned earlier. They want to know their purpose. This indicates that much work remains to be done for us to be a purpose-driven people. Pastor Yvonne and I want to share with you what we have learned so you can grow in your own self-awareness. We want to help you as you embark on or continue your purpose quest. We invite you to connect with us now as we share how our connection with one another and the purpose message has furthered the concept of purpose in the lives of people all over the world. We are confident your connection with the purpose message and with us will give you your own unique stories as well. Let's get started.

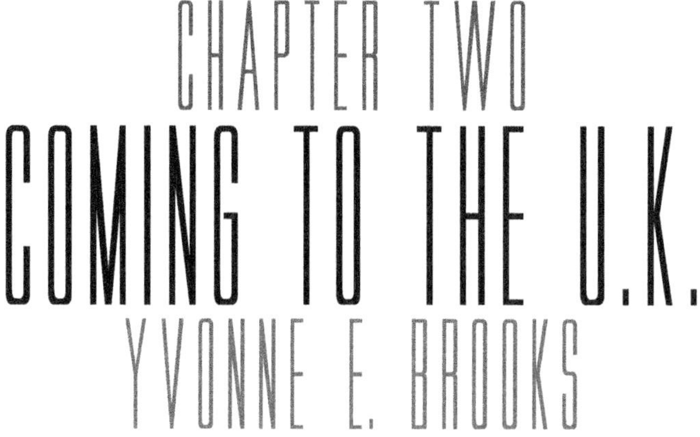

I was born in Jamaica where we adored everything that came from England, our mother country. We loved the Queen and the royal family. Someone only had to say Britain and everyone would stand at attention and feel special. Therefore, when Britain sent out invitations for people to come there and work, my parents decided they would go for just a few years and then return home. My father was a carpenter and was quite gifted, even able to make his own furniture. When he got to the U.K., however, he found himself earning less than what he was earning in Jamaica. Plus, my parents found that the people in the U.K. were not that nice. In the windows of some of the houses for rent, people like me would see notices that read *no blacks, no Irish, and no dogs*. Thus, it was difficult for my parents to find somewhere to live.

When we joined my parents in 1964, my mother

was providing foster care for a little girl from her church because no children were allowed in the house where her parents lived. That meant the family only saw their daughter on Sundays when they went to church, and my mother kept the child for the rest of the week.

My parents were ambitious, so they were actually able to save money under those conditions. They made the most of what they had, were frugal, and worked together as a team. I mentioned my mother was a foster parent and my father did the things he could to make our lives comfortable. For instance, he gathered waste bits of carpet from the jobs he performed and made a carpet for our house. Most people at that time did not have sitting carpets; they would only have a rug, but we had a fully-fitted carpet because of my father's craftsmanship and creativity. It meant we were warm in the house because of it.

In my family, I am number five of eight children, and when my parents came to the U.K., they left five of us in the West Indies with my grandmother. Their plan was to send for all of us later and they did eventually send for my brother (number four of eight) and me, which meant my three sisters were left behind. One was not well, one was at university studying to be a teacher, and the other had started her family, so they never made it to the U.K.

Back in those days in Jamaica, we children had a carefree existence but of course there were challenges. One of the things we experienced as children of parents who left us behind was the cruelty of those still in Jamaica. A lot of the other children, plus some of the grownups, were vindictive towards us. They would call us names and start fights with us. At that time, I used to have a slate instead of a notebook with a slate pencil and a special carrier bag for my slate.

Every Monday morning, I would go to school with a new slate, and by Monday afternoon that the slate would be broken by some vindictive child who felt that our parents were in England and therefore thought we were better than they were. That was their way of trying to bring us down a peg or two. I would refuse to go to school with a broken slate, and therefore missed a lot of school because my grandmother could not force me to go. Then one day, the good news came that I was going to England to join my parents. Of course, in my child's mind, I thought England was just around the corner.

I was eight years old at the time and I had no idea I was going to have to get on an airplane and travel eleven hours to the U.K. That was a strange experience. Before we left, we had to go around the district where we lived to say farewell to everybody. There is one thing Jamaicans do well, and that is train their children to have good manners and to respect anybody that is even a day older than they are. When we went around and said goodbye to the neighbors, they all gave us a shilling, a half a crown, or some amount of money as a farewell present to help us on our way. For the first time in my life, I felt really rich.

It was at this time that I discovered I had a middle name. I was not just Yvonne Clark; I was actually Yvonne Elizabeth Clark. The next thing I discovered was I had a birthday. No one had ever told me I had a birthday and we had never celebrated it in all of my eight years. Because I was traveling, it was possible that someone would ask me when I got to England when I was born. Therefore, I needed to know my full name and how to spell it, along with my birthdate. That was a very exciting time. I got on the airplane, and there was a bag in the pocket on the back of the seat in front of me. I put all of my money in there, not realizing it was an airsick bag. The hostess collected it, thinking it was rubbish, so I lost all my money before I even arrived. I was quite upset.

We eventually got to England where we had to wait a long time at the airport. I had never felt cold like that in my whole life. I was dressed in a nice short-sleeve summer dress, and I knew I looked great because it was my favorite color—yellow. When we got to the airplane exit, I wanted to rush back into the plane because we were so cold. They had to wrap us in two blankets each before we went to the hall to wait for my father to pick us up. After about four hours, there was no sign of him, but someone made the decision to put us on a bus that would take us to Victoria Station. We were confused because we had never been to England, had never been cold, and did not know if our father would be there to meet us.

When we got onto the bus, the driver wanted us to pay the bus fare. My money was gone so we could not pay, but he said he would collect it when our father came to get us. When the doors opened, we were relieved to see my father and another man with him, who I found out afterwards was his pastor, had come to collect us. This was the happiest day of my life. The only reason I knew he was my father was everyday my grandmother would show me his picture and say, "This is Richard Clark, your father." I knew every part of his face, so when I saw him, I leapt into his arms. We laughed and cried at the same time. That was how I began my life in the U.K. I was freezing cold, but happy to see my father who I never recalled meeting in person before that day.

When I first arrived, I missed my grandmother because she was the only mother figure I could remember. My brother and I cried so much that if my parents had the money, I am sure they would have sent us back to Jamaica. Of course, now I am quite glad they did not send me back because of the opportunities I have been exposed to, the education I received, and the people I have been able to meet here in the U.K. Those things would never have happened had I remained in Jamaica.

In fact, as I have grown older, I have recognized how often God was working my life and I was not even aware of it. What's more, He was always working for good to prepare me so I could connect with and fulfill my purpose. In the next chapter, I want to tell you about my preparation years after I arrived in the U.K. Let's go there now.

CHAPTER THREE
THE SCHOOL YEARS
YVONNE E. BROOKS

At first, everything in the U.K. frightened me. Once I was going to the hospital with my mother, and a train let out a screech as it came to a stop. I broke away from my mother and ran. I was accustomed to the life and sounds of the Jamaican countryside, so I thought something was coming to get me and I was terrified. The loudest sound I had ever heard before that was a car horn. There I was in a big U.K. city where we also experienced smoke and smog from the chimneys along with the fog, and everything looked so dirty. We would go out, come back home, and our faces were covered with soot, because people warmed their homes with a coal fire and the smoke was nasty and everywhere.

My parents were Christians and were living in a house with their pastor. It was a four-story house and they had two rooms on the bottom floor, which today would be called a basement. In those two rooms lived my three brothers, the young girl who my mother was fostering, my parents, and I. On Sunday, my mother would get a lift to church and take one of the children, but the rest would have to get on the bus with my father. The church was in Stonebridge Park, which is near Wembley Stadium. It required three buses to get to church or back home, so we usually did not get back home until dinner time. Some of the other saints would take us to their house and feed us. Then we would go back to evening service and make the long trip back home at night.

We went straight to school after four days of being in the U.K. Assimilation was not easy because my mother had some funny ideas. For example, the school informed us that we needed a PE kit, so my mother gave me what are called bloomers, which were ladies underwear that came down to my knees. If we did not have a PE kit, we had to take off our clothes and have PE in our vest and knickers. Imagine me in a lady's vest and bloomers, doing PE with the other kids. There were not many other black kids in the school, so we immediately became targets and the other kids would take the mickey out of us. They would do anything they could do to make the other kids laugh at us—and my mother always seemed to give them what they needed to mock me.

My mother made us wear hats to school, and we had better come home with the hat. The girls would grab my hat and throw it from one girl to another, with me running in between them trying to get my hat back. They did not realize I had a bad temper and so I got involved in many fights, usually beating up the girls. Eventually, they left me alone, but it was a really hard season because despite my bad temper, I was a friendly and outgoing girl. I expected to make friends, but all I seemed to do was make enemies because I was so different than my classmates.

There were no white people in Jamaica, but since we revered everything British, we did not expect any discrimination in the U.K. After all, we were all fellow citizens of the British Empire. Not everyone, however, shared our sentiments. I certainly did not expect to be treated any differently, so it was a huge shock when people actually started picking on us because we were black. They called us golliwogs and told us to go back to where we had come from.

After being at that school for a few months, my parents saved enough money to buy a house of their own. My dad had gone around to view houses, but when the owners saw he was black, they would lie and say the house was already sold. My dad was clever, however, so he got a white workmate to go with him and pretended that the white man was buying the house. That man did all the paperwork for my father until it came time for him to sign and then my father signed. After that, it was too late for the owners to pull out of the deal. That's how he got our first house, which was at 151 Wells House Road.

When we moved into that house, I thought only our family was going to live there, but my mother and father took the front bedroom upstairs and then they used a second bedroom for my brother. Then the third upstairs bedroom and the front room downstairs were rented out to others because that's how black people managed to live back then. They had to share with other black people, because whites were not renting them rooms. Therefore, we ended up with five different families in our three-bedroom house.

The school in this area was much better because there were a few more black kids—not many, but a few. I went to a primary school, which I really enjoyed because I was in a class with another black girl. Her family was from Grenada and she was given charge to look after me and to ensure I was okay. When I started my lessons at the new school, we had only learnt to write in cursive, and the teacher said I must stop using that since it was too advanced for my age group. I still blame that teacher for the terrible handwriting I have. Apart from that, I did really well.

I will never forget Mr. Cobbley for as long as I live. He was a great teacher and made such an impression on me because he encouraged me to read, and I was so inspired that I sometimes would read three books a week. When he saw how much I was reading, he advised me to join the library, informing me that my mother would have to sign the card so I could join and borrow books. I did not know if my mother would do that, but when I asked her, she signed. It was a mobile library that came to our street every Wednesday afternoon when I would go and choose three books.

Because I was a girl, my parents would not allow me to play out on the street. I had to do my housework and homework for school and stay in the house. Once I had those books, I loved staying in and read copiously. I started off with fiction, then historical fiction, and on to history books about King Charles I, King Charles II, Lady Clementine, and other people in history. I could not do enough reading.

The next thing I started to read was my Bible, and I found it quite interesting as well. By the age of 11, I had given my heart to the Lord. Of course, I attended Sunday School every Sunday morning, then morning service, and then evening service as well. Mondays we had choir practice, Tuesday was prayer meeting and Bible study, and Wednesday we had other church activities. Thursday was another time of Bible study. Friday was young people's meeting and Saturday we would clean the church and get ready to start the routine all over again. My life was busy with schoolwork, reading, and church, which did not allow me time to make or keep many friends. My mother always insisted that friends would get me into trouble, which was the reason I was better off staying to myself. Despite her warning, I did manage to have one or two friends, who I still have up to this day.

Jackie Bryan was one friend, and she was such a nice English girl. After she made friends with me, I would go to her house at lunchtime, but I could never tell my mother. She would also invite me to tea sometimes at her house after school. I knew if I accepted the invitation, I was going to have to endure a beating when I got home because my mother would want to know at 5:30 where I had been and why I was not home at 4:00. It was so worth it, however, and I was friends with Jackline until I was about 18. After we left school, we went in opposite directions.

After leaving home to get married, I put a great value on friendship, and try to make some new friends every year. I work to keep the old ones, but also make the effort to develop at least three new friends who I can carry forward with me in life. I realized that life is so much better when we have good friendships with people who will tell us the truth and not allow us to labor under false ideas or allow us to misrepresent ourselves.

As you probably surmised, my mother was very strict, but I realized later in life that she was just trying to protect us and did that in the only way she knew. She did not pursue other methods or ways because she felt her ways were the best ways. I had a silly childhood notion that these were not my real parents because they were so strict, and I wondered when my real parents would come get me. It was only later in my adult life that I realized they did the best they could. I came to this realisation when I took a family systems course and through that course I was able to completely forgive my parents and release any grudges I had against them.

While I realized they did the best they could, I also

concluded that the best they could do was not the best for me as an adult. I learned if I was not careful, I could end up doing the same things as my parents. I could not do what they had done and feel it was acceptable or good enough; I had to do better because more knowledge and information were available. Why would I want my own children to have the same experience as I had? I was able to change quite a bit of my thinking and my approach to life and parenting.

I can look back now and see how God's hand was guiding my life decisions after I finished school and pursued a career. I am telling you this so you know for sure that I had no special advantage in life that gave me an inside track to success or purpose. If I found purpose, you can, too. In the next chapter, I will tell you how I got into the nursing profession, the next step in my purpose journey.

CHAPTER FOUR

MY PROFESSION AND MARRIAGE

YVONNE E. BROOKS

After school was over, I worked a temporary job as a receptionist in the West End while I was waiting to start my nurse's training when I turned 18. By then, I had a few friends at church. One was Patricia Diedrick, and we are still friends. My all-time best friend who is still my friend today is Eileen Mitchell. She is totally amazing and is the person I turn to when I need counsel, advice, or just someone to listen. Because she is a year older than I, I benefited from all her castoffs like her handbags, shoes, and dresses, and that allowed me to look a bit better than I used to. Eileen would also take time to show me how to do hair styles. In fact, she was the one who got me dressed for my wedding day and was my chief bridesmaid.

One of my sisters became a teacher, so by default it was decided (and don't ask me how since I was not at the meeting) that I would become a nurse. My mother refused to allow me to work in a factory, insisting I must earn some kind of professional qualifications. My teachers informed me that I needed to gain four 'O' levels in order to get into Hammersmith Hospital, which was one of the leading post-graduate schools of nursing. I wanted to get into that school because it had such a great reputation. When I first went to my career advisor to inform her of my decision, she laughed me to scorn, not believing I could do it. What she did not realize was that was exactly the motivation I needed. When anyone told me I could not do something, then they only had to sit and watch me do it because I had learned to work and defy all the odds.

By the age of 16, I pushed and studied and worked really hard. I stayed at school until I was almost 18 years old, and I actually got my O levels so I could do my nurse's training. It's really humorous to me now, because the same teacher who did not believe I could do it had become the deputy headmistress. When I was in my third year of training, I went back to the school to see them, and she paraded me around the whole school as if I was her prize pupil, telling everyone how great I had done.

By that time, I had already taken my hospital exams, comprised of two five-hour exams, as well as four assessments throughout my training. I passed my hospital exam and was waiting to do my state exams. She asked me to come back and say something at an assembly to inspire some of the other youth, which I did. I got through my nurse training, which lasted for three years, and qualified as a state registered nurse—which the headmistress had told me I would not be able to do, mainly because I was black. Maybe she thought I was stupid as well. My registration was as a mental health nurse, doubly qualified in two fields, and I worked in the mental health field for 27 years—after which I became a full-time pastor.

In 1970, Melvin, my future husband, came to the U.K. from Jamaica. At that time, we held young people's monthly meetings in the church organization of which we were members, and we would go all over the country for these meetings. Every month throughout the year, the young people would meet together, and I met Melvin at one of these meetings when he came straight up to me to introduce himself. I had never seen him before but he seemed like a nice guy and had very good manners (of course he did, he was Jamaican). I was only about 17, so I was not allowed to have a boyfriend, so I was not particularly interested.

A group of us started to be pen pals, and he was one of the group along with six other people. Over time, everyone dropped out, except for Melvin. He kept writing but keep in mind that communication was not as easy as it is today with phones, texting, and WhatsApp. We did not even have a phone in our house although there was a public phone box on our street, which we used. We had no choice but to use letters and telegrams. Melvin and I would write and during that time we found out a lot about each other. He always encouraged me in what I was doing, and I guess he always thought that one day we would get married—and one day we did. I was 21 and 8 months old when we tied the knot.

If you speak to him now, he would say he was called to be a pastor then, but I had no idea at the time because I did not want to marry a pastor. I wanted someone who would sit next to me in church, hold my hand, look into my eyes, and be romantic. The day after we got married, I found out he was a deacon, but was still not impressed. After being a deacon, he became a minister, then an elder. Today, he is a bishop, but that was not in my plans at all.

When we first married, Melvin was working at GC National as supervisor in their stocks department. He was the stock controller for all the things they needed to make the meters and measuring equipment, including gold, silver and other metals. He had to be quite regulated in how these supplies came in and went out because, of course, gold and silver are precious metals and people would try to steal them. He worked full time Monday through Friday and sometimes on a Saturday.

After a month of being married, I started working at a mental hospital doing my mental health nurse's training, which lasted 18 months. Of course, we were very involved with church meetings up and down the country. I was actually a missionary in the church and would run meetings, and became the women's meeting coordinator responsible for all the meetings. At that time, I was singing in the choir and responsible for choir practice, which included learning new songs, choosing and caring for the uniforms, and other administrative types of things.

When I joined my parents in England as an eight-year-old, I remember our home being filled with music. The choice of music was limited, but I only realised that as I got older. I listened to singers like Mahalia Jackson, Mario Lanzo, Jim Reeves, and Jacky Edward. My parents were proud of their musical collection and, especially on weekends, their albums would flow through our home and out through the open windows. This was a reflection of the musical inclinations of both my parents who sang in churches and choirs long before I was born. In our local church, my mum and dad sang as part of the main church choir, the men's/women's choirs, a quartet, and any other group ranging in size from two to the choir. Growing up in this environment, I found singing was as natural as breathing. I thought it was like that in every-one's home.

I too joined in the singing and would burst into songs just like in the musicals. Up to this stage, the singing consisted mainly of the songs I learned like a parrot from the albums and hymns from church, or sometimes one of the other young people at church would have a song they would teach and share with us.

My life changed when I visited my friend at her home to listen to a new album she had purchased. It featured someone named Aretha Franklin. I couldn't believe the sounds she made with her voice or the fantastic music that accompanied her in songs like *O Mary, Don't You Weep* and *How I Got Over*. Of course, my friend refused to loan me her record and I went home with only what I could remember.

About that time, I discovered a few new artists. The one that has been the most impacting for the past 42 years was Andre Crouch and the Disciples. From the moment I heard *Take Me Back*. I discovered a new level of gospel music. He was the first man on a poster to make it into my bedroom. I attended Andre's concert at the Hammersmith Odeon with my mother in 1977 and after that, I followed them around. My brother, Bobby Clarke, was the drummer in a group called Paradise and they were the warmup act for nearly all Andre's concerts in the U.K. Most of Andre Crouch's songs became my songs as I sang in duos, choirs, and other groups. I can remember key events in my life based on the songs he made popular at the time.

In our family we would sing at home as a whole family, too. My mother became the choir leader for the young people's choir at the church and every week all the young people would come around to our home for choir practise. We would plug in the electric guitars and sing to our heart's content. Thank goodness we had understanding neighbours. In church services, the entire Clarke family would sing group songs. My brother, who hasn't been in church for more than 30 years, still sings these songs because they make him happy. I use singing like medication; it lifts my spirit when I am down. When I need to extract everything out of a moment, singing or listening to songs helps me get into a specific place or mindset. I would sing with another group of four girls as well, and also went all around the country singing in our young people's services. To this day, I'm still known for my singing even though I hardly sing anymore.

I imparted this love for music to my children as well. If you think the atmosphere that I grew up in was full of singing, their atmosphere was even more so. Our family singing started in earnest out of necessity. Adam was five or six, and Rebecca was seven or eight when we started coming to Birmingham for all the church services. There were no musicians, so we filled plastic bottles with pebbles and shook them like maracas. We had a tambourine and that was the only music we had in the church. Then Adam started sitting behind the piano and playing with two fingers, and Rebecca became our first worship leader.

We sang in the home and always had a piano in the house. My brother was a drummer and so he inspired my son Matthew to play. My other brother played around with the keyboard and Adam got that interest from him. Rebecca began to sing when she was only two years old, and has never stopped. The children began to lead the worship in the church and are still doing it now. Their sound was birthed out of their grandparents and also their parents, even though their dad was not a wonderful singer.

Even now if I go back to my church in London, they will talk to me about my singing and my mother's singing, because my parents were always on the choir.

In fact, that's where the legacy of singing comes from. My mother used to sing in a group of older people, and she was a soloist who was in demand. Everywhere she went, she would be asked to sing, so it came naturally for me. My only regret is that I did not sing more with my mother. We sang a few songs together, but we could have done more.

Let me tell you about my children's arrival since I have already mentioned their musical role in the church. I was 23 when I gave birth my first child, Rebecca. Within the first few hours after she was born, I realized I was a mother for a lifetime! I remember being head-over-heels in love with this amazing child. She was the first grandchild in my husband's family, and the second grandchild in this country for my parents. Therefore, she was spoiled and surrounded with adults, and thought she was the same age with the same privileges as the adults. That is probably why she was so confident to start singing in front of a crowd at such an early age.

Then when she was three years and three months old, I gave birth to Adam. He weighed nine pounds, five ounces, while Rebecca had been seven pounds, four ounces. I was not satisfied still and knew I wanted another baby. When I was pregnant with Matthew, I looked like I was twenty months pregnant when I was only six months along. I could not lie down on my back or on my side because the weight was just too much to bear. The doctor estimated the baby would be about ten pounds in weight. When he was born on July 27, 1998, he weighed in at twelve pounds, four ounces so I had to have a C-Section to deliver.

During his birth, I was given nine units of blood. That scared me because this was the time when the AIDS epidemic was at its highest. I did not even know they had given them to me because I was unconscious. I was frightened and convinced they were going to tell me I had contracted AIDS through the blood transfusions—but thank God that never happened. The doctors thought something was wrong with the baby because he was so big, but when they examined him, they found nothing wrong. People stopped me in the street so they could see the size of this baby. All he did for 12 weeks was eat and sleep. He was so contented, and I was happy, but I knew then there would not be any more babies because the doctor said if I had another one, he or she would be probably weigh about 15 pounds.

I had been working as a nurse throughout my pregnancies. I was on full-time day shifts in the beginning, but by the time I had Matthew, I was working two nights as well—while still going to church and helping Melvin even more. After I had Matthew, I stayed in Stafford and went to church there, even though Melvin had been sent to Birmingham. I wanted to be in the same church with him, however, so I went with him so I could teach Sunday School and lead the service. Then I would usually catch a train back to Stafford and go to work on Sunday night. Eventually, we attended a church-growth seminar and discovered that we needed to send follow-up letters and make phone calls to visitors who came to the church. I started to do all that—following up with people and inviting people to church, while trying to make the services more interesting.

When I was a nurse, I used to say to God. *Why am I working here?* I was working in the mental health nursing community and I felt that I was giving so much to my work and it was not really appreciated. I felt I would be so much more appreciated in church. Now many years later, I find that it actually is not true. Whatever we do, we have to do unto the Lord because He is the only one who will appreciate it. People will always see what we're doing in a different light than we see it and often don't understand (or don't care) what it may cost us to do it. I would say,

Lord, why am I working at the mental health desk when I want to be in full-time ministry? Don't You want me to be in full-time ministry? He said, "I am preparing you for full-time ministry. That's why you are working with mentally-challenged people."

That was the best preparation ever because everybody is normal until we get to know them. I believe He gave me the right background I needed. I was the full-time breadwinner after Melvin went into full-time ministry in 1998 and the church could only afford to pay him £100 a month at first. After a couple years, it went up to about £300 a month.

I wasn't making a lot of money at that time, maybe £1,000 a month. God turned our money into elastic, however, and stretched it beyond what we thought possible. What should have been one of our hardest times was actually a time of greater productivity in our personal lives, in our financial lives, and in the church life than whenever we were both earning a lot of money. We saw God's hand provide for us time and time again. Let me give you an example.

We realized we needed to move from Stafford to Birmingham. We did not know how we were going to do it because Melvin was just earning £200 a month and I was taking home £1,000 a month, and we needed to get a new mortgage to move. Prior to that, we had had an accident in the car six or seven years earlier, and for some reason (we don't know why), they offered us a settlement at the time. I turned it down because it was an insult. What's more, they wanted us to pay a fee for a consultant to sort out the claim. Therefore, we left it alone for six years.

Finally, the company got back in touch with us because the time to settle the claim was running out. They asked if we wanted to proceed, but I said we still didn't have the money for the consultant. They then said they would pay for the consultant and get reimbursed from the other party, which we felt they should have done in the first place.

We had been trying to sell our house in Stafford and we never managed to sell the house. This year we put it on the market, within two weeks the house was sold. In a couple of months, we had to move out but had nowhere to go. We had to move in with friends in Birmingham and then within a matter of four weeks, God delivered us into our hands the house we are in now, which is our most expensive house to date.

He put everything together for us to get the mortgage. There was a shortfall and at that time, the money from the accident compensation came through at the right time and enabled us to put enough money towards it so we could obtain the mortgage and buy everything new for the house. Over the next couple of years, God stretched our money so what would have been normally a hard and difficult time became a time of God's provision. It was a confirmation that Melvin had done the right thing by stepping into full-time ministry. To us, it showed God's hand that He was with us. We moved into the house in 2000.

In 2004, I left my full-time job to go into ministry. I worked for my employer four days and I worked for the church one day throughout 2004. Then God helped the church grow, and slowly we were able to receive a better salary between the two of us. God has provided for us up till now. That was my transition into full-time ministry, but it was not without preparation. It was not without God saying, *I'm the One who controls timing. Don't rush ahead of Me. Don't think that you know more than I because you don't know what's ahead.*

I was busy with one foot in two worlds—nursing and church work. That divide would continue for many years, until I connected with the message of how to find one's life purpose and then everything changed. It was then, when I learned to accept who I was and who God made me to be that I was able to celebrate and embrace my call. Let's move on to that part of my story next.

CHAPTER FIVE
BEING MYSELF
YVONNE E. BROOKS

The first church I attended when I came to the U.K. conditioned me to think that I could not be myself. The church had a long list of things we could not do, as opposed to what we actually could do, so we were never quite sure we were doing the right things. Everyone disapproved of something, so we tended to do as little as possible so we would not incur the wrath of God—or the other saints. The leaders told me if I was baptized, I would go to heaven. I did not want to die and go to hell but wanted to go to heaven. That was the main reason I got baptized when I was eleven because I did not want to go to hell. Then after I got baptized, they told me I needed to be filled with the Holy Spirit, and I thought, *My God, they've changed the rules. Now I need to be filled with the Holy Spirit.*

The problem was that to be filled with the Holy

Spirit, I thought I had to be holy and perfect, which was impossible even for an eleven-year-old girl. I was convinced there was nothing I could do that was good enough. I had a mental picture of God as an old man with a long white beard and a huge stick, and the stick was poised, ready to hit me any time I moved out of my assigned place or did something wrong. I was not motivated by love. They keep saying that God is love, but we were never acquainted with this part of God and we seldom had that modeled for us in real life. We were only acquainted with Him as a disciplinarian, who was waiting to get His revenge by beating the heck out of us. Therefore, I never really got on to the right page with Him at a young age.

I was about 18 or 19 years old when a visiting speaker came and taught us about the love of God. Through that narrow window, I had my first ray of light and hope that it was quite possible He loved me and that is why He gave Himself for me. I started reading my Bible more at that stage and tried to have conversations with other young people at church to see what they thought. We were quite enthusiastic young people at that time. It was great to be in a group who also seemed to be going in the same direction and pursuing the same spiritual things.

From there, I actually started paying more attention in church. No one could speak to me when the message was being presented. They knew not even to try, because I wanted to hear what the speaker had to say. I made a serious effort to know God and thought that maybe there was a future in Christianity for me. I actually fell in love with God, but I still had this image in the back of my mind of Him being someone who was more than willing to knock the hell out of me. The fact that God actually recognized me as an individual person who cared about me as a human being never occurred to me before I was about 29. That's where my mind was.

I had a sense for a while that God was directing me to do something with and for women when I realized that many women were coming to me with their ministry and marital issues and problems. I wondered why they were coming to me because I did not have a history of doing such work in ministry and did not have an established ministry of my own. In fact, both my husband and I were rather new to pastoral ministry.

Melvin had been sent to pastor the church in Birmingham just after we had our first child. The church was small, made up of three or four adults and several Sunday School children. We wanted the church to grow but in hindsight, I realised that if everyone had the same problems as I did, the church would never grow. Even though I had grown up in church and had been on various choirs and really wanted to make it happen. I didn't realise there was a purpose for me being here on the earth. It always seemed to me that there must be more to life than being born, getting married, buying a house, having children, and then dying. The dots were not yet joined up for me nor was there any understanding of what part I would play in it. I heard the word *purpose* a few times, but it not connect with me. Certainly, important people like ministers, pastors, and bishops probably had purpose but who was I to have purpose? That was above my station in life.

As I said previously, we really wanted the church to grow. We decided to have a revival service and looked around to see who we would invite to speak. Eventually, my brother-in-law Benjiman suggested a friend he had in Youngstown Ohio, USA. We found out what we needed to do to have a guest speaker and everyone at the church contributed to the expenses of having him come. He came and was kind enough to stay at our home rather than in a hotel, which would have been more expense. He brought an encouraging message and was really fun to be with. He was a happy child of God and exhibited hope and excitement in his future and the future of the Church. He was married to a beautiful lady named Angela and they had two young daughters. When he left us, we were firm friends.

He spoke about concepts like abundant life and he even had an acronym for LIFE: Living In Fulfilled Expectation. He talked about the power of God working in our lives and he opened my eyes to the fact that each individual is known and loved by God. That meant that I was personally known and loved by God. This knowledge reduced me to tears and a longing to be used by God began to rise in my heart.

Within two months, Elder Glenn Brady was back again after he suggested we hold an Abundant Life Seminar. We didn't know about this before he introduced it to us, but just the name got us excited. We invited everyone we knew to attend that one-day seminar. The theme was "From the Pew to Performance" and his message for the day was all about purpose, and he demonstrated that the power in every church was already sitting on the pew. We needed to step into and fulfill God's purpose for our lives.

I sat through the teaching that day, mesmerised by the words I was hearing that fueled a surge of life in a way I had never previously experienced. The *more* I had been looking for had come to me as he spoke the words that we were born on purpose, for purpose, and with purpose. There was a reason why I was here on planet Earth. God actually knew I was here and had created my purpose first, then created me to fulfil that purpose. I carried something from Him that I would need to use in fulfilling my God-given purpose.

I had heard great messages being preached before this but always felt there was a huge gap between where

I was and where the messages told me I needed to be. There was great possibility in Christ but I never knew how to get there. Nowhere was I presented with the how of what I needed to do.

I felt as though I had been born again into a new world with different possibilities and a new trajectory. My outlook was changing. I felt closer to God than I had ever felt. I had to work on maintaining my new mind-set where I saw a loving Father rather than a task master waiting for me to get it wrong.

Whilst he was with us, Elder Brady persuaded us that we should attend a conference that his pastor, Bishop Norman L Wagner, hosted called "Pentecost in Perspective." He invited us to stay at his home and within one month we were in Youngstown, Ohio in the U.S. We were excited and arrived on a Monday. Tuesday evening, we went to Bible class, which was packed with people. As Bishop Wagner taught and prepared us for the conference, he told us we were not there by chance but by the deliberate move of God. He told us we should listen and be aware of the move of God. We were told to "expect God."

My anticipation grew as Wednesday drew nearer when the conference was to begin. When it began on Wednesday morning, I had never been in an atmosphere like that. There was so much happening, not just in the natural but especially in the spiritual realm. I had never before heard anyone speak like Bishop Wagner. He spoke not only of possibility but of actuality. He spoke about things that had happened, some of which he caused through his prayer, pronouncements, and faith. The whole experience was on a different level than we were accustomed, and I spent the next four days having my paradigm not just shifted but totally smashed and re-arranged.

The day sessions were held at the church, and

we were taught and challenged by speakers like Elaine Shouse-Waller, Wanda Davis-Turner, and others from the church itself. The different kinds of people who were attending and all the information I was taking in were life-changing. The evening sessions were held in the Powers Auditorium in downtown Youngstown. During one of the evening sessions, the speaker was Bishop T.D. Jakes whose wife had just had their fifth baby. It was exciting to hear him speak and everyone was on their feet as he finished. There was a large contingent from the United Kingdom, so I knew the change was not just for me but for the U.K. as a whole since the various people would bring back and put into action what they had received.

The next significant step for me was when I met a gentleman named Dr. John Stanko. I was attending a conference some friends in Watford had organised. We had choices as to which teaching session we attended and I chose to attend Dr. Stanko's teaching. I was fascinated as I listened to his teaching about purpose and his mention of personality profiles.

I had always had issues around my personality, because I was told I wasn't serious enough. It seemed to me that to be a proper Christian, one had to be serious, maybe even a bit miserable, with a look like one had been baptised in lemon juice. I liked jokes, I had a sense of humour, and loved to laugh. Sometimes I would teach or preach, and in those times, I felt like I had to be someone who was serious and somewhat harsh. I realise now that the Scripture really is true when it says, "as a man thinketh in his heart so is he" (Proverbs 23:7). How I thought about myself affected the way I saw others. We had always sung a lot of songs about being free and having our chains broken, but in reality, freedom was a limited commodity. I had an appointment sometime later with Dr. Stanko to take a personality profile. It was a little scary because I didn't know if it was a test and if it was, I could fail. What if I failed my own personality test? What would I do?

Dr. Stanko assured me it wasn't a test I could fail and so I went forward. It consisted of a booklet with a set of questions (which I needed to answer without too much deliberation), a graph page, and then a write up on each of the personality styles that included how the styles was represented in the life and actions of Jesus. Once I had answered all the questions, the score was done, and the graph mapped out.

Dr. Stanko then gave me the detailed feedback and insights into what my results meant. I came out as a High-I style, which I will discuss more at length in another chapter. This helped me understand that God had made me with this bubbly personality and therefore He must have a use for it. I understood that there was no blame for having a sense of humour and loving laughter, but it was actually deliberate on God's part. It was many years later that I got a great insight whilst I was speaking at a Women's Aglow Meeting. The ladies were laughing and as they were laughing whilst I was teaching, I had the strongest impression that they were being delivered from a variety of things. They were being freed from pain, fear, disappointment, loneliness and more. When speaking with the ladies afterwards, they were kind enough to share with me what they had experienced during the time I was teaching.

God had given me a great sense of humour and sense of empathy so He could use it for His purpose. I had no idea that God was so deliberate and intentional. Over the years, my favourite verse was any version of Jeremiah 29:11, "I know the thoughts I think towards you, saith the Lord, thoughts of peace, and not evil, to give you an expected end" (KJV). I had read Scripture before believing it for others, but not quite seeing that it applied to me. This verse I believed and embraced to the core of my being, holding on to it in good and bad times.

I don't go back any longer to the church I grew up in because we are not allowed to wear earrings and makeup there and when they see me wearing them, they think I have backslidden. I only go back for a funeral or an event for someone I knew well. To me, hearing the purpose message was when I really connected with a loving Father. Now let me go back and share more about how Women of Purpose came into being, for the purpose message was soon to have a new home in the U.K. in an organization I helped birth and develop.

CHAPTER SIX
WOMEN OF PURPOSE
YVONNE E. BROOKS

I don't know how God speaks to other people, but it literally feels for me like He delivers a little package of the Word to my mind. He dropped an idea into my mind that I needed to start something to cater to women and minister to their needs. At the beginning, I did not have a name for the ministry I wanted to do that was directed toward women. I conducted a few one-day seminars and conferences, and one of them was called *Everything's All Right at Home*, which was aimed at ministry wives, encouraging them to make sure their homes and husbands were cared for before they embarked on the road for ministry. I would field question after question about how to go into ministry. Don't ask me how I knew the answer because I did not even feel I was in ministry at the time.

From those one-day events, I felt pressure to do something more organized. I spoke with my sisters-in-law,

Lorna and Avril, and they suggested a few other ladies to include, and we started to meet together and pray. We decided to name what we were doing Women In the Word. Pentecostals, especially the black segment, did not have many social outlets or expressions, especially when it came to Christmas or other special times of the year. The first thing we decided to do was hold a banquet at Christmas time to which we invited women.

We booked a hotel in Birmingham called the Wesley Hotel even though we had no money and told the hotel we wanted 100 places set for the banquet. They said the Christmas tree would be up, the place would be decorated, and there would be no extra charges for that. We chose a beautiful menu and decided to go to the next level and hire a four-piece orchestra to play for the ladies in the background. I did not even have a dress I could wear to a banquet so I had to borrow one. I was standing at the door when the women started to come in.

The ladies were dressed in style with hair done, jewelry on, and I thought, *Oh my God, who are these people?* Then I started to recognize some of the women who were members of my church, others were members from other churches, and 100 women showed up. We encouraged them to have a great evening. At that time, I was working as a mental health nurse and one of my patient's husbands was a photographer, so he volunteered to take our photographs, develop them, and get them back to us within a week. All the ladies had their photographs taken.

We gathered around the tables and had our meal with the orchestra playing in the background. It just so happened that the very same weekend, Angela Brady was visiting from Youngstown, Ohio, so we asked her to be our speaker for the evening. She was a very beautiful and elegant lady, and she brought something special to the evening. Everything was absolutely perfect. The ladies raved about the evening because that was the first time in our history that something like that had happened. It was so beautiful and the year was 1998.

After we finished that banquet, the committee members were so excited that we decided to go ahead and press on to host our first conference. This was daunting to me because I had not attended that many conferences. I did not know how we should structure it, things like the planning, the agenda, or even how to get a speaker. It was all unknown to me.

We had our planning meeting and one of the ladies said she knew someone we could have for our speaker. It was a woman I had met when I was in Youngstown, Ohio. I approached her and asked her if she would speak, and she said the Lord had already spoken to her and would be glad to come. I also invited two other ladies to the conference from the U.S. and we set the date for April of 1999. That was our first conference.

We decided to meet in Shrewsbury, 30 or 40 miles from Birmingham, even though at the time I was still living in Stafford. We met in an old stately home that had been redesigned as a conference center. The stables of the home had been converted into the conference rooms. We could tell they had been the stables because we could still smell the horses.

As we organised, I asked the Lord. *How will we get people to come because nobody really knows me? Who's going to pay money to come?* We had calculated it was going to cost 120 pounds per lady, which would include accommodations, food, and other expenses and we had spaces for up to 120 ladies. To my surprise, everywhere I went to advertise, I boldly told the people, "God said you have *got* to show up." Those seemed to be the magic words because then people would ask me for a booking form. *How do we sign up? How do I pay? Can I pay in installments?* As we went along through the months, we started to build momentum as people paid. We decided on the theme, which was "Thy Kingdom Come."

Around Easter time, we booked a coach so people could travel together who were coming from out of town. We had come from all different places in the country like London, Reading, Birmingham, and Wolverhampton. It was all beyond my experience, so I really did not know what to expect. We went ahead and anointed every chair in the conference room. We prayed through the whole building, including the bedrooms, and invited God's presence to come. We decorated the main room by draping fabric. I also invited a few pastor's wives to come and support me because my knees were knocking and my teeth were chattering—I was really nervous because I did not know what I was doing. It was nerve-racking for me, but the women came.

We started on a Thursday morning and went through Saturday afternoon. One hundred twenty women turned up and we had our first session, which was a "trashing" session, which was the time I felt we needed to get rid of everything that was hindering or preventing us from going where God wanted us to go. Our speakers had been charged to speak in a given area of the conference theme, which was "Thy Kingdom Come." We knew times of prayer had to be a big part of the conference. We were all sitting in the conference sessions with our hats on like it was a Sunday service. We did not realize God was going to walk in and set aside all of our tradition and the things we were hanging on to for security.

From the first moment the conference started, the worship was totally amazing. We were able to get a woman by the name of Marcia Fothergil to come and play the keyboard. It was low profile, but it was as if everything was amplified. It seemed like in my mind that everything was on loudspeaker. We started off with a couple of ladies leading the worship and from the very first song, the presence of God fell. The place was like a big cauldron of worship. Everyone was worshiping, even though we did not all know each other. We had three or four speakers who all did a fabulous job.

The pastors had shown me great trust because in those days, a lot of those pastors did not allow their people to go anywhere because they were afraid their parishioners would be poached. I assume the ladies asked permission, or maybe they just came anyway. The women were so hungry for what God was doing and from that first song the limitations were broken off. We saw miracles happening in the ministry of healing and deliverance.

A couple of ladies whose husband had told them they could not come came anyway. One man got his wife's clothes. poured kerosene on them, and burnt them to prevent her from coming. All she had left were the clothes she had brought to the conference. There was that type of warfare against the conference, but it was as if God said, *Okay, I will meet that resistance with My overcoming power.* If you ask me what the overriding theme of the conference was, I would say it was that many women were given a mantle of authority for ministry.

Up to that point in our churches, we were taught that only men could go forth in ministry. Only men could be ordained as ministers, leaders, and pastors, and women would do the kitchen work or teach Sunday School. Most assumed they did not have the potential, nor was it God's will for them to rise up in ministry. In that conference, we saw the Holy Spirit falling on the women and I could literally see mantles of ministry, authority, and anointing being placed on them.

When our guest speaker spoke, she led us on a spiritual adventure. She took us to places in God we had never experienced in God. For the first time, we saw the possibility of God working in our lives, and the things

He would do and the spiritual warfare that we would wage against the powers of darkness through us. She also showed us that we needed deliverance to be a daily witness by the way we lived so God's kingdom could be manifest and resident in our lives.

She was totally awesome. She showed us how to stand together as women, urging us to have each other's back. She taught us that we needed to pray for and support one another. She got the women to believe in themselves because God had a plan for their lives, and that was the most awesome result of all. Nearly every woman left that conference feeling like they were able to step out in ministry, in little or larger ways. She showed us that we could not remain the same as we were when we first showed up at the conference.

When I left that conference, I thought it was the only conference we were ever going to have. By the time I got home, the Lord had spoken to me, giving me the theme for the following year, which was "Thy Will Be Done." Therefore, we began planning for the next one. The following year, we also did a program called *Who Do You Think We Are?*, which was a one-day conference. Keep in mind, the women had left the first conference believing they needed to step out in God, believing Him for their ministry. A lot of people were asked that question whenever they went back home, *Who Do You Think You Are?*, so we held the one-day conference addressing that question.

That was our pattern for the ladies for the next few years. We would have a conference, a seminar, and then a banquet each year. At the same time, we were publishing a magazine called *On Purpose*. The first edition was called the "Now Testament" and was printed in a four-color magazine format. Before that, it was a newsletter we would photocopy and staple together ourselves.

My music gifts then became part of the

conferences, even though I did not think they were very significant. It really helped in those early days when we did not have a lot of help. After two or three years, my entire family started coming to conference. Adam ran the sound system and Matthew would play the drums while Adam also played the keyboards. Of course, Rebecca would lead the worship. They actually took us deeper and deeper into worship. Even now, I still sing at conference. A lot of people who only got to know me recently are surprised that I can sing so well, but they don't know my history of singing.

The next April we had our second conference. They were all the Women In the Word conferences, which we kept doing for the next few years. We started to increase and soon outgrew the Christian conference centers, so we ended up going to hotels, which were more expensive. That began to raise the standards I felt God wanted from us. It was about the sixth conference when a man named Dr. John Stanko came to our event. That's when we changed the name from Women In the Word to Women of Purpose.

I have written enough for now, so let's hear from Dr. Stanko and read what he has to say to us about purpose. This is the message that changed my life, so let's tune in together for the next chapter, for I know what he writes has the power to change your life as well.

CHAPTER SEVEN
MY PURPOSE CONNECTION
JOHN W. STANKO

As I was reading Pastor Yvonne's manuscript, I was intrigued by her purpose story and journey—some of which I knew and some I learned for the first time. I thought, *That's what I should do in this chapter. I will include my own purpose story alongside hers.* I went into my books and articles on purpose to find something I could copy and paste for this chapter my purpose testimony, for surely it existed somewhere in the volumes I have written.

Alas, I was mistaken and that was quite a surprise to me. While I have told my story hundreds of times, while I have written about parts of the story in many places, I could not find my entire story in one place. That isn't right, so I am going to correct that error right here and now by telling you my purpose story from the beginning, which for me was 1991 (I know I said I was not going to get into ancient history, but please indulge me just this once. I won't do it again.).

In 1991, my pastor came to me with a group of men who had an idea for a business that involved selling advertising for an attachment that went under a landline phone (I told you this was ancient history; who has a landline phone these days?). Since I had a master's degree in economics, they asked me to lead the business team, promising me a $30,000 salary once things got rolling—which I was assured was just a matter of time.

That was all I needed to move into high gear. We signed a lease for office space and a phone system, got office equipment and furniture, and hired a few sales-people. We had meetings where we established a business plan (complete with Bible verses, I might add) and prayed elaborate prayers with eyes closed and hands held high, signs of our earnestness and fervor. When we dedicated the office complex to God's glory, a pastor came and heaved globs of anointing oil all over the place when he prayed, which we didn't clean off the walls. The oil that slowly moved its way down the walls was only a visible symbol of our certain anointing—or so we thought.

There was only one problem: through all our efforts and my organizational skills, God never got the message we were even in business. In only nine months, we were out of money and had only a few prospects signed up for the service. All those people who formed a circle and held hands to fervently pray began to jump ship and before I knew it, I was the only one left to try and salvage the business. To make matters worse, my name was on all the leases. (We did not have time to incorporate, so as the team leader, I used my signature to guarantee payment.)

The Bible says when we pray to find a quiet place or a closet and I certainly felt led to pray because I was left holding the bag for a lot of lease payments. The quietest place I knew was our business office (the phones never rang and no one ever came by), so I went one morning to ask, no to *plead* with God to save the business. As I sat behind my desk, I raised my hands in prayer (not real high, just shoulder height), closed my eyes, and prayed this prayer, "Oh Lord, save this business for Your glory!" When I got to the word glory, I needed something special, something that would give the prayer more pizazz when it reached God's ears. That's when I thought of a woman in a former church we had called the Glory Lady.

This woman was in the first church I attended after I came to the Lord. She sat in the last row and had hair stacked up on top of her head that took on the shape of a cone or what we used to refer to as a dunce cap. When she liked something going on in church—a prayer, a message, an exhortation—she would say "Glory!" but she said it with a voice lower than the Dead Sea and with the same amount of vibrato every time: "Gloooooooorrrrryyyyy!" On that morning in my office, my prayer needed a boost, so I copied the Glory Lady's style and said, "Lord, save this business for Your gloooooooorrrrryyyyy." I thought I had done well.

As soon as my prayer was finished, this thought came through my mind: "You're not interested in God's glory; you just want to save your own neck." That was true. I was praying a religious prayer because I thought it would work best, but if I was to be truthful, I was angry and upset that God did not help me in this business endeavor. I had done all I knew to do but it ended in failure, and I was not a happy man. I opened my eyes, lowered my hands, and pounded my desk, shouting, "If You didn't create me to start this business, what did you create me to do?" Keep in mind, I wasn't looking for information; I was simply venting my anger toward God.

To my surprise, my mind immediately went to Genesis 1:2. I wasn't thinking about or reading the Bible, I hadn't been reading Genesis, and I wasn't in the mood for a Bible study. Yet I had no choice but to go to Genesis since the impression was quite strong, and there I read, "Now the earth was formless and empty, darkness was over the surface of the deep, and the Spirit of God was hovering over the waters." Don't ask me why, but I had a Bible commentary in the office and I got it off the shelf to read what it had to say about this verse. The author had written the following: "The Spirit was there to bring order out of chaos."

Order out of chaos.

That morning, in the midst of my confusion and anger, I now realize I had found my life's purpose. All throughout my young life (I was 31 at the time), I had loved to organize. As an eight-year-old, I would clean out my father's garage, taking everything out, hose it down, and put everything back. When I was done, I would stand in the middle of the garage and have this inexplicable sense of peace and joy. I would replicate that experience wherever I was—in school, at play, and later in my first jobs. I set things in order that were in anything but order and then have a sense of accomplishment.

I didn't know what to do with what I learned that morning after my "gloooooooorrrrryyyyyy" prayer, so I didn't do anything. I reflected, read, and studied what "order out of chaos" meant and concluded that I had indeed found my purpose. I also assumed if I had a purpose, then others did too, but I didn't know the implications for that realization in my life—until I moved to Orlando, Florida in 1989 to pastor a church. In addition to the church, I led a prison ministry that met weekly with a discipleship group of inmates.

I decided to experiment with a purpose message I had developed with my prison discipleship group and the men were intrigued. That led to some great, insightful discussions that kept alive my interest in helping others find purpose. I also shared some of the concepts with my small home group in Orlando, and I saw the makings of a nicely developed message on how to find life purpose.

It was then that I was invited to help my friends at Integrity Music develop a worship weekend seminar. We agreed that I should teach on leadership while I was there, so I premiered a message titled "Effectiveness: Finding Your Life Purpose." The rest is history as I have gone on to deliver that message more than 1,000 times in many countries, including sessions in Birmingham and London at the invitation of my friend, Yvonne Brooks.

What are the lessons from my purpose story that can and will help you with your purpose? Let's look at a few:

1. Your purpose is summarized in one simple statement that has profound meaning for your life only. It is usually accompanied by a verse or passage from the Bible that describes or depicts what the statement means.

2. Most people don't know their purpose because they don't ask and keep on asking.

3. Sometimes we don't ask because we don't really believe we will receive an answer. If I found an answer and I wasn't even looking for one, how much more will you receive an answer from God if you seek with honest, faith-filled intent?

4. Once people find purpose, they often want to know what to do next. I didn't do anything when I discovered mine, but instead

spent time (years actually) meditating on what I heard and praying about what it meant. God wants you to know and fulfill your purpose more than you. You are not alone, and God will help you all along the way to know what to do once you know who you are.

5. Many people want to know how their purpose will translate into income because they start to think how their purpose will express itself. If that's you, my advice is to focus on the *what* it is you are supposed to do and not think about money, which only complicates and discourages the process of finding purpose. If you are to write, then write, and don't get bogged down in who will publish or buy what you write.

6. Once you find purpose, you will often be called upon by others to help them find theirs.

The purpose message is what I brought to the U.K. that caused Pastor Yvonne to adjust the name of her organization from Women In the Word to Women of Purpose. What an honor it was to be involved in those early days and now to be reconnected to the ministry once again. Let's move on to the next chapter to look at another aspect of my ministry that made a deep connection in the hearts of the women in those early conferences and ministry visits, and that is the subject of personality.

CHAPTER EIGHT
PURPOSE AND PERSONALITY
YVONNE E. BROOKS

As I mentioned in chapter four, Dr. Stanko introduced the personality DISC profile and people's lives were changed because of being exposed to that profiling. Women continue to testify of how the profiles impacted their lives and gave them so much meaning. That was the main reason why I changed the name from Women In the Word to Women of Purpose, because I felt that was the track God wanted us to be on.

Then Dr. Stanko started something in 2001 called the *Monday Memo,* a weekly email letter to encourage us in our purpose. In fact, he announced he was going to start writing it when he was at our church, and people enrolled who were interested in receiving it. He has sent 920 weekly *Memos* since then to people all over the world, and it has been a lifechanging thing. I know people who print them off every week and have folders full of *Monday Memos.* It impacted them because there was someone who regularly spoke and wrote in practical, everyday language. He was someone who was able to laugh at himself as opposed to himself, which flew in the face of our idea that we were children of God and therefore had to be serious and never joke.

After I met Dr. John Stanko, he eventually introduced me to the DISC profile. He pointed out that my personality, strengths, and weaknesses were not an accident; God made me the way I am. God had given me my personality and He had use for it. When the lightbulb of that truth went on, it was quite cathartic for me. It was almost too good to be true. He backed it up by doing the DISC profile. The DISC said that I was a High-I style (intuitive, inspirational, spontaneous, needing many relationships to be fulfilled, good in front of a crowd) with very little S, a little D, and very little C.

At first, I did not know how to take that, but then I realized, *Oh my God, that's describing me to a T.* It was not abnormal to be like this, but God wanted to and can use me. The DISC profile booklet described Jesus' personality when He functioned as an I-type person. He was accessible to everyone, could teach all day, and loved to be around people. That led me to understand more about who I am and why I experienced some of the feelings I had throughout my life. I would feel so excited about something and someone would come along and pour cold water on it, and I would plunge into the depths of despair. High-I styles tend to have high highs and low lows.

I learned my High-I type did not want to be in a

rut or a routine in which things were the same for 365 days a year. I like new things and realized that I was a good starter. I'm not always a good finisher, but I can initiate and birth things. Dr. Stanko advised me that I needed a team of people around me who had the styles I did not have. That way we could work together and be an effective team, complementing one another. All of the styles could then come into play as each person fulfilled and expressed their part as they were purposed to do.

That was life-changing for me. I saw myself differently and that brought me into a new place. Then I redid my profile many years later, and I came to see that I had some D (director, wanting and needing to be in front and in charge, bored with the mundane, quick to come to conclusions) and a little bit of C (compliant, given to details and procedures, methodical). I always felt like I had no C because I did not want to pay attention to details. I discovered that when the pressure is on, I can be the most detailed person in the world. As you can see, the DISC profile was like a window that allowed me to see parts of myself I did not know were there or existed.

For many years, I had a desire to be in full-time ministry. At some point, I thought it was absolutely pointless and futile. Because I was moving forward but my feet were not going anywhere. When I tried to fill my cup, my cup had a hole in it and everything leaked out. The day Dr. Stanko came, the purpose message and profiles plugged the holes.

I would often agonize and think, *God, choose someone else. They are more qualified. That person is better looking. That person has more experience.* As I began to accept each part of myself, I became a more rounded and complete person. I am not so hard on myself. Sometimes I respond automatically, but when I take the time to think, I can really sparkle. I accepted what God saw in me and the fact that He knew me as an individual and had plans for my life that only I could fulfill—as He created me to be, not as someone I was pretending to be. After that moment of insight into who I am, however, I realized that even with my lack of experience, God wanted to use me. There was a significant shift in my spirit and my thinking.

I don't think Dr. Stanko fully understands what a deep and lasting impact he has had on my life. Before he came along, nobody ever said to me the things he said. It happened not only when he spoke directly to me in our private sessions. Sometimes it would be part of his teaching, but he did not know how I embraced those words and hid them in my heart because they gave me life and direction. It gave me a reason to be alive and to keep on going.

I also came to realize that God does everything right on time and that He always prepares us before He releases us into any given area—whether it's marriage, full-time ministry, or a new career. He does not want us to fail; he wants to set us up for success. I needed to hear the message Dr. Stanko carried and he came in God's perfect timing, and now I am trying to do the same for others.

I don't take any salary from Women of Purpose or The Esther Academy because we sow any profit back into the ministry so we can reach other women. I'm hoping that at some stage I can receive some money from it. If that was possible, I would not split my time between the church and Women of Purpose. If Women of Purpose could pay part of my salary and the church pay another part of my salary, it would ease any burden on the church. It would also allow the church to employ a few other people.

The good thing is that we do already have a few Purpose Partners who give regularly. It's not very much, but they do give regularly. What we need to work on is increasing the number of people. I also realize that when people's circumstances change, one of the first things they cut is giving to ministries. I would prefer for us to have things for Women of Purpose and Esther's Academy, whether it's books or some kind of merchandise we can actually sell that will actually bring in an income.

I haven't received any words to describe what I feel the Lord wants to do through my purpose. I have a feeling inside me that's rising up—a story or a song, but something big is supposed to happen. I need to be challenged on a regular basis because I can get comfortable saying, "Yes, I'm doing well," while there is so much more to do and be, based on the ability God has given me. I have the ability to do more, so why am I not doing it? What's holding me back? What's going to be my excuse?

I took a team of six ladies to South Africa three or four years ago and we trained 25 pastors with the Esther program. We have four academies running at the moment and this started from those six ladies. We traveled, shared, and even mentored the ladies. It's been absolutely amazing and the most satisfying thing in the world. We made mistakes, but we have learned more from our mistakes than if we had remained sitting on the sidelines.

Let me stop here and allow Dr. Stanko to share from his perspective on personality, for I know his encounter with the DISC profile was as significant as mine was, and I know you will be encouraged by what he writes. Let's hear from him again.

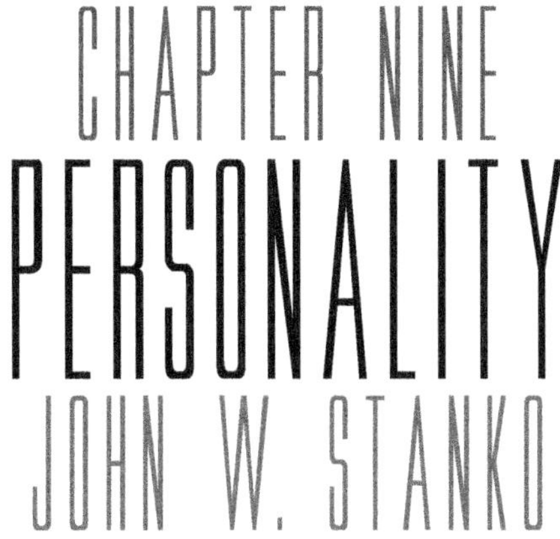

Pastor Yvonne refers frequently to the DISC profile and the impact it had on her life. I can say the same thing, for God used the profile to help me understand who I am (and who I am not), which helped me identify my purpose and avoid distractions. I was so impacted by the profile in 1992 that I said to the Lord, "This was such a blessing. I would like to become certified and, if You will help me, use what I know to help other people." I did, He did, and I have. That is the reason I introduced the profiles to Pastor Yvonne and the other women because I know how much we struggle as believers to talk about our strengths and weaknesses. The profiles help "prime the pump," so to speak, and get us in the flow of discussing our God-given personalities. Let me tell you more of my story so you will understand why and how the profile made such a difference.

In 1974 after graduate school and while working as a financial aid officer for a chain of trade schools, I started to prepare for the ministry. My pastor began to mentor me and expose me to the things I would need to be a successful pastor. I eventually enrolled in a seminary and received a masters and doctorate in pastoral ministries. In 1989, I became pastor of Covenant Church in Orlando, Florida, and pastored that church for four years. I was finally where I wanted and thought I was supposed to be.

There was only one problem. I found out that I didn't like pastoring. More than that, I discovered that pastoring didn't like me. I was a task-oriented individual functioning in a career and position that required a lot of people-oriented skills. While those skills could be (and were) learned, they still took a lot of energy and generated a lot of stress, for they did not come naturally for me. I wasn't a happy leader because I wasn't leading where I could utilize my strengths to the fullest.

At the urging of a friend, I completed a profile called "The Personality System" published by The Institute for Motivational Living, Inc., in New Castle, Pennsylvania. This profile is also known by the acronym DISC, because it identifies four behavioral styles that begin with the letters DISC. The D stands for dominant, driving, determined; the I for influencing, insightful, inspirational; the S for steady, stable, secure; and the C for compliant, correct, and conscientious.

My original profile results clearly showed that I was under tremendous stress and pressure trying to be all styles to all people. That's what the ministry can do to someone who feels the pressure to adapt to everyone's expectations, something I was trying to do to be a "good" pastor. The profile went on to show that I was a "C" style with a "D" as a secondary style. I was a task-oriented individual who liked projects and tasks and the challenges that came with them.

The profile indicated I was quite low in the "I" style and also low in the "S" style. In short, I functioned best in situations that required strong administrative and organizational skills, and less so in situations that required a lot of interpersonal contact and nurture. I wasn't cut out to be what I call a Sunday pastor.

Armed with that information, I resigned (after much soul searching, for I had thought all my life that it was what I was supposed to do) the pastorate to take a job with Integrity Music as director of their conference and educational division. That began three of the happiest and most fulfilling years of my life. Whenever I have gone back in church work over the years, I'm more knowledgeable of who I am and who I'm not. I still do pastoral things, but I avoid being drawn into all the activities of the pastorate and maintain a good percentage of my time in the areas of administration, project management, writing, traveling, and team building.

That DISC profile caused me to look at who I was and wasn't. It's not magic nor is it perfect or psychologically sophisticated. It was enough, however, to get me started on a path of self-understanding that has enhanced my leadership abilities. I stopped trying to be what I wasn't and began to strengthen and improve what I was. As Jesus said, "You will know the truth, and the truth will set you free" (John 8:32). I connected with the truth of who I am, and as promised, I was set free.

Also, you remember that Pastor Yvonne is predominantly a High-I style, and I am a High-D and C style. That means we can work well together as a team because we are so different. We complement one another, but we have to work to understand each other, for we will approach a common project or idea from totally different perspectives. It requires us to communicate clearly and precisely, for it is easy for a High-I and a High-C to hear through the filter of their own style and that can cause problems. So far, we have been able to avoid any difficulties because we have good self-knowledge.

Peter Drucker's book, *Management Challenges for the 21st Century*, addresses the issue of self-knowledge. Drucker encourages leaders to develop feedback analysis. This is done "whenever one makes a key decision, and whenever one does a key action, one writes down what one expects will happen. And nine or twelve months later one then feeds back from results or expectations" (Peter F. Drucker, *Management Challenges for the 21st Century*. New York: Harper Collins; 1999; page 164). From this, Drucker summarizes three *action conclusions* from the feedback analysis:

1. **Concentrate on your strengths**. Place yourself where your strengths can produce the results from your strengths.

2. **Work on improving your strengths**. The feedback analysis rapidly shows where a person needs to improve skills or has to acquire new knowledge. It will show where skills and knowledge are no longer adequate and have to be updated. It will also pinpoint gaps in your knowledge.

3. **Work to correct *disabling ignorance***. This he describes as areas of weakness that undermine one's strengths. (Peter F. Drucker, *Management Challenges for the 21st Century*. New York: Harper Collins; 1999; page 165-167)

My profile not only helped me to identify my strengths but also to work on my own disabling ignorance. While my profile showed my task orientation, it also revealed how little I understood people who weren't like me, coupled with a paltry comprehension of where they were "coming from." That would have been true of my work with Pastor Yvonne. Before the profile, I would have avoided working with someone like her because that person wasn't organized enough for me. Those people were too "flighty," going from one project to the next, while I preferred to drill down deep, take my time, and finish what was started. I realized how rough I could be working with people who were motivated by relationship or routine—that represented my disabling ignorance.

I began to work on understanding what motivated people who were not like me and began to apply what I learned. I was still motivated by my strength of getting the job done, but I was complementing that strength by learning how to motivate people and win their support. In this way, I made my strengths of project management fully productive. I've had to improve my people skills if I was going to be fully productive because the projects I oversee all involve people. To not do that would be to render my strengths useless or less than they could be, and that wasn't acceptable to me.

In knowing myself, I've come to some other conclusions about who I am and am not. I've discovered that:

1. I love to travel, partly because of the challenge it presents that satisfies my "D" style and partly because it gives me uninterrupted chunks of time to read, write, and work on projects that require more focus.

2. I can work with people, but when I do, I need to schedule some "down time" somewhere after we're done to replenish and recharge my batteries.

3. I am a morning person, working best in the early hours on writing and projects. I need to leave busy work, phone calls, meetings, and follow up work for the afternoon.

4. I like working for a big organization where there are lots of activities and opportunities.

5. I'm a city person. I like traffic, people, and activity. The mountains or nature hold no special blessing for me.

6. I prefer to listen as a way to learn, but I don't mind reading. For me, it's not either/or.

I've included those few personal likes and dislikes to show that I've worked on who I am, worked on knowing myself. I'm still learning, but I've taken seriously Drucker's challenge to self-knowledge:

> We will have to learn where we belong, what our strengths are, what we have to learn so that we get the full benefit from it, where our defects are, what we are not good at, where we belong, what our values are. For the first time in human history, we will have to learn to take responsibility for managing ourselves. And as I said, this is probably a much bigger change than any technology—a change in the human condition. Nobody teaches it—no school, no college—and [it] probably will be another hundred years before they teach it.

> In the meantime, the achievers—and I don't mean the millionaires, but rather the ones who want to make a contribution, who want to lead a fulfilling life, and want to feel that there is some purpose in their being on this earth—will have to learn something which, only a few years ago, a very few super achievers ever knew. They will have to learn to manage themselves, to build on their strengths, to build on their values. (Peter F. Drucker, quoted

from the Closing Plenary Session of the 1999 Leadership and Management Conference in Los Angeles, California, November 9, 1999).

Do what you must do to learn about who you are and aren't. Build on your strengths and minimize your weaknesses. Don't rely on charisma or special talents to prop up your leadership position. Work to know yourself and then improve from that base of knowledge. That is what I have come to love and appreciate about Pastor Yvonne. She is totally committed to the self-knowledge and self-awareness process, and she works to better understand who she is and what makes her tick. That's why she has been so successful, and why I enjoy our working relationship. She is my alter ego and I have learned as much from her as she claims she has from me.

While I am on a roll, let me address something else that has joined Pastor Yvonne and me over the years and that is the topic of creativity. Let's go there in the next chapter.

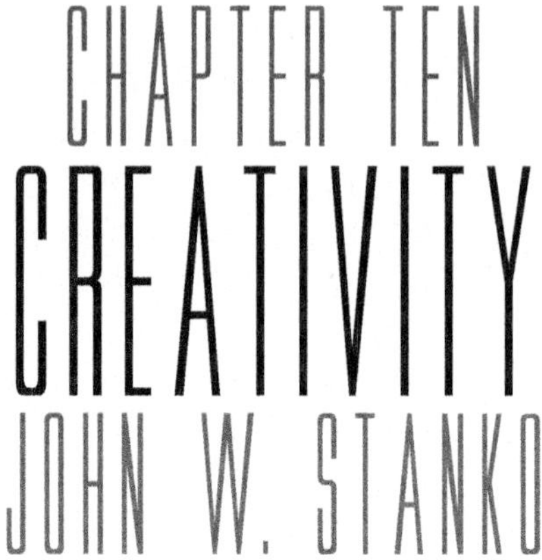

I don't think Pastor Yvonne has mentioned creativity specifically in her story, but it is implied throughout. Her musical ability is certainly part of her creativity as is her tremendous sense of humor. When she founded Women In the Word and renamed it Women of Purpose, it was also an expression of her creativity. The Esther Academy is again a result of her ability to create something out of nothing, and her fertile mind coupled with her High-I personality style are always producing thoughts of doing new things in fresh, innovative ways.

I write this chapter on creativity because of its importance in finding and fulfilling life purpose. When I first described my purpose, it was "to bring order out of chaos." I want you to keep the word *bring* in mind as I proceed. Over the course of my adult career, I did not see myself as a creative person and would say so. I thought of myself as an administrator who could fix problems but not as a creator who could start new things. My thinking was that creativity was conceiving of or doing something the world had never seen before, sort of like Einstein who came up with a formula that no one else had ever produced or imagined.

Then one day in 2005, I was in Zimbabwe driving to the church where I was consulting, and had, for lack of a better term, a significant spiritual experience. I was thinking about the concept of creativity when the Lord spoke to me: "You don't *bring* order out of chaos, you *create* order out of chaos. You *are* a creative person!" It was as if the Lord was in the car with me. I heard an audible voice so clearly that I turned around to make sure there was no one in the backseat. *I was a creative person. I am creative!* Those thoughts flooded my mind and I can still see my hands trembling on the steering wheel.

My experience did not end when I arrived at the office, for I kept thinking about what I had heard and continued to tremble throughout the day. Then as I settled down, I reflected on my life and began to see that the declaration was indeed true: I had been and was a creative person. I had started playing violin when I was eight years old and became quite proficient. I did not have a lot of friends to play with, so I found ways to play by myself. I created a baseball league and would throw a ball against the stone wall at our home, actually pretending that two teams were playing one another. I would field the ball as it came off the wall, or at times it would fly over my head, but each throw and resulting bounce back counted as outs or runs. I kept score, maintained the standings of wins and losses, and had playoffs at the end of the summer before school began. I was creative!

Then as an adult, I was an event planner, a writer (of letters and assigned articles, never anything on my own initiative), and a humorist (I had been able to make people laugh from the time I was four years old, so I know where Pastor Yvonne is coming from in her journey to make peace with that side of her personality). I saw that all those were creative expressions. When I heard the voice in 2005, I had started two companies, written six books, consulted, coached, advised, developed workshops and seminars, and had championed the purpose message along with a message on servant leadership through my writing and speaking, something few other believers were doing as I was.

This revelation changed my life and the way I saw myself, and I was so excited that I knew I had to share what I had learned with my following through the *Monday Memo*, my blog, and my online Bible studies (which, by the way, were other creative expressions). Who was the first one I heard from when I started writing on creativity? It was none other than Pastor Yvonne, who said I must come to the U.K. to teach on creativity, and that is of course how she responded when she first heard my purpose message.

I developed a seminar, Pastor Yvonne booked the Hilton Hotel by Wembley Stadium, and we had a number of people come to that event. This was just another example of how Pastor Yvonne and I were "joined at the hip," always together and thinking about how to share what we were learning with our followers, readers, and listeners.

There was one other event that she reminded me of recently and that was the launch of my purpose coaching service. I cannot remember the exact year, but I invited her to come to Dallas where I was launching my *Seven Steps of a PurposeQuest* seminar. After the seminar, I enrolled people in my coaching program and it is still one of the more significant and profitable things I have ever done. I issued an open invitation for people to come to my opening event, and Pastor Yvonne was the first to respond. During her time here in the States, we had a chance to visit Bishop T.D. Jakes at his church, which only made the weekend in Dallas more memorable. How could I have forgotten that?

As I look back, I am not surprised that I had an epiphany where creativity is concerned. It seems like once people overcome their hesitancy and fear to find and express their purpose, creativity is not far behind. It's like purpose is locked up in a cage, and when they open the door, creativity jumps out before the cage door is closed. I was coaching one woman to help her find purpose and we made great progress. Then one day, she said, "I have some poems. They're not very good but I have written them over the years and never shown them to anyone. Could I show them to you?"

When I asked her how many poems she had, she replied, "Hundreds." When I read them, they were quite good and she has taken steps to use them more in her ministry, but she is not ready to publish them yet. My point is that creativity is often connected to purpose, for people of purpose will find new, fresh ways to do what it is they were created to do. That is what I have done, for I have invented many new approaches and programs to help others create order out of their chaos and find purpose.

The concept of creativity is found in the earliest part of the Old Testament, Genesis 2 to be exact. It is there that God directed Adam's work but allowed Adam to express his creativity:

> Now the Lord God had formed out of the ground all the wild animals and all the birds in the sky. He brought them to the man to see what he would name them; and whatever the man called each living creature, that was its name. So the man gave names to all the livestock, the birds in the sky and all the wild animals. But for Adam no suitable helper was

found (Genesis 2:19-20).

I have discovered that we as believers are a bit ambivalent about our role and God's role in creativity. We are fearful of doing something outside of God's will, so we often describe our creativity as purely a function of God's leadership. Therefore, I hear people say when talking about their creative expressions, "The Lord spoke to me; the Lord directed me; the Lord laid this on my heart; God inspired me; God told me to do this or that," always careful not to indicate any personal initiative in what they did.

I believe God does "speak, direct, lay on hearts, and inspire" but I don't believe He does that for every creative expression. Otherwise, we are simply robots or secretaries taking down God's dictation. If you have a six-line poem, does God have to be the One who initiated that? Is it possible for you to decide to express your creativity and then do it? Part of the problem is our fear of failure, of misrepresenting God, of seeming like we have an ego or self-will.

In Genesis 2, God did not bring an animal to Adam, only to have Adam stare at it dumbfounded, at which point God whispered in his ear, "Cow," to which Adam said, "Cow. We will name this a cow," to have God respond, "Good job, Adam!" That is not what happened, and if it did, it would not have been Adam's creativity. There is no question that the Fall marred and polluted mankind's creativity, but Jesus came to reconcile all things to the Father, and that includes our creativity. We can be creative and *not* be outside of God's will, *unless* we commandeer our creativity to use solely as we see fit, not making it available to God's direction and use.

Since I accepted the adjustment in my purpose statement from "bringing" order to "creating" order, my creativity has exploded. I now have 45 books to my credit, including two fiction and eleven volumes of a verse-by-verse New Testament commentary. I maintain four Facebook pages, write every day, posted a daily devotional online for seven years (*every* day), and started a publishing company called Urban Press, which is the publisher for this book and those of others.

I started the publishing company to help people express their creativity when it jumped out of the cage as I described earlier. I sit with people to develop and edit their manuscripts, and I hold their hand as they navigate the minefield of creative expression. I have seen people produce a completed book manuscript, only to have them get cold feet just as we were about to publish, and the main culprit was fear—the same enemy trying to prevent them from finding purpose. Even in this project, Pastor Yvonne and I have collaborated, and I have had to encourage her, even though she is much more creative than I am. The only difference is that I have learned to face and manage my fear, which is something she is still learning to do.

Pastor Yvonne mentioned something I have written since 2001 called *The Monday Memo*. I developed the *Memo* in response to many people who would hear my purpose message and then say, "We need more help. We wish we had you around more to talk to so we could bounce things off you to see if we are on the right track." Also, I was about to launch a website and thought, *What reason would anyone have to come to my website except to check it out when it launches?* I thought I would write the *Memo* so every week people would be reminded of the purpose message and could then access the many resources on my site. As of this writing, I have written 920 *Monday Memos* (my goal is to reach 1,000).

At first, I was afraid (yes, there is fear again) I would run out of material or get bored or, worse yet, the readers would get tired of it. To my surprise, none of that has happened. It has been a great exercise in faith to sit down every Sunday night for more than 18 years and trust God to help me produce something to help people everywhere find and fulfill their purpose. I have also written about my travels, creativity, leadership, and faith (just to name a few of the other topics), and the feedback has been phenomenal and a source of encouragement in my creativity work.

In my next chapter (after we hear from Pastor Yvonne), I will share a few *Monday Memos* with you that are pertinent to this book, but also to give you an idea of what they look like to stimulate your creativity. You will see that each *Memo* is only six or seven paragraphs, so they are pretty short and to the point. I have turned many of the *Memos* into books, which allowed me to work smarter by achieving two objectives while I wrote one *Memo.*

Let's look at a few of them in my next chapter. I want you to pray as you read them, "Lord, how can I take what I know and who I am and share that with the world?" This is one way God may want to put you on the world stage, which I know is an objective of Women of Purpose. As you pray, I know God will help you take the next step to express your creativity as you confront your fears of doing so.

CHAPTER ELEVEN

PURPOSE POINTS

YVONNE E. BROOKS

Today, I try to evaluate everything I do through a purpose grid. There are more things in my life that need to come under that type of evaluation, but my mantra today is on purpose, for purpose, and with purpose. We're not random beings. Dr. Stanko helped me to see that my uniqueness is deliberate and purposeful, and God wants to use it all.

As I told you, I knew nothing about purpose, even though I grew up in church. I felt that our purpose was just to go to church on Sunday, Tuesday, Wednesday, and Friday evenings and then pay our tithes and offerings. As long as we did that, we would please God and get into heaven.

That's one of the first things I was able to get rid of when I encountered the purpose message, first through Elder Brady and then in more detail from Dr. Stanko. The former was teaching it in general, but Dr. Stanko ministered it to me personally. He spoke to that person in me who was looking for something but did not even though she was looking for.

The other thing I have learned over the years is purpose is not just for Christians. Every human being is looking for purpose, significance, and meaning, and God even speaks to those people as their God. As Christians, we may think we have got the exclusive right and ability to hear from God. I believe God speaks to everyone, but we as believers should hear more often and clearly because we have a relationship with God, and we have the Holy Spirit to help us hear and then obey what we hear.

I also realized not too long ago that we will never feel God's approval and affirmation if we do not step out into our purpose. Every time I do what God is directing me to do, it seems somebody then comes along to tell me how inadequate I am and how I'm going about it the wrong way.

Recently in the face of that reality, I stood up and did what I felt God wanted me to do. As I stood there, I have to describe it as a feeling similar to a warm glow. I felt His arms around me and heard Him saying, "You can do it because I have given you the power and ability to do it." I felt affirmed and encouraged because He allowed me to see that I no longer needed to listen to people who dismissed me or discouraged me for whatever reason. It is not strangers who discourage us when it comes to purpose. It is often the people who we know and are closest to us. Instead of encouraging and affirming us, they often try to talk us out of what we are thinking, perhaps because they don't believe it possible and are trying to protect us from the pain of disappointment.

I looked up the definition of *purpose* in the Oxford English dictionary and found it to be "the reason something is done or created or for which something exists or a person's sense of resolve or determination." Purpose or a sense of purpose is intrinsic to each human being. It's not just part of being a Christian; purpose is for everyone. There is a problem God wants to solve or a need He wants to meet, and that is the reason He created human beings with purpose, talents, and gifts. God did not try to find a solution or an answer for it. He's already created the solution to it before the problem even manifested—and that's where you and I come in.

Most people I meet are searching for purpose and some sort of meaning in their lives, even if they have never heard the word purpose. They know they are looking for something that's going to shift the balance in their life from boredom to meaning. They're looking for something to make them feel like they are part of something greater than they are. God does not work randomly, but is deliberate and intentional about what He does. That is what helped me see that purpose began for each of us before we existed.

As an eight-year-old child, I remember seeing a television for the first time. The program I remember watching was *Peyton Place*. I started wondering if life was like that TV show. *Were we all just actors in a play, and if so, who is directing the play? How would it end?* I had these kinds of questions at a young age. I never saw myself as important or thought there was something specific that I had to do. It was many years later before I discovered that in God's eyes each of us is unique and possesses gifts, talents, and abilities that can make a demonstrable difference in the world.

I eventually concluded that everything about me was deliberately designed and put together to bring glory to God. Even my sense of humor and fun was to bring glory to God. That was amazing and enlightening to me. It is easier to talk about that than actually do it. Even though I am well down the road of my purpose quest, which I did in conjunction with the teaching Dr. Stanko gave me, I had to battle all of the obstacles of the past and the old mindset. I had to do more positive things and surround myself with positive people. I had to listen to recordings and teachings to help me become who I was learning I was designed to be.

That is when I developed a new awareness of my responsibility to God, and even to humankind. God was depending upon me, but there were also other people who were depending on me to play my part. It's like a play. If somebody does not follow the script, design the scenery, hire the actors, or promote and sell the tickets, the play will never happen. A lot of the productions we see on Broadway would never take place. The trajectory of my life and my part in the lives of others would not take place if I did not play my part, whatever that part is. Once again, I recognized the call of God on my life and accepted the assignment. Once I did that, I noticed that God began to speak to me in new and fresh ways. He opened doors and sent mentors.

Another thing I have realized in my purpose journey is that a mentor does not necessarily need to be alive. They can mentor you from the beyond the grave through their books, writings, or audio recordings. People who are alive can mentor me also, but I may never meet them but still follow what they have done and their example and experiences and then apply those lessons to my life.

None of us can achieve anything without proper mentors. God does not expect us to operate in a vacuum. He becomes our first partner in our purpose quest to fulfill the call on our lives. Not only does He partner with us, but He releases the resources we need to do it. I have discovered with each new assignment that I also attract God's provision as I act. When God works in our lives, He appoints us to bear fruit. He chose us for good works that He has promised will remain and be long-standing.

He gives us knowledge of who he is. He also gives us knowledge of who we are.

As I pursued my purpose quest with God, he turned the spotlight on me so I could see me. When that happened, I could see some of the things He had placed in me. When He tests us with hard times, it's never so He can get an answer or find out some information. It's always so we can know the strength He has built into us. I got some very good advice from one of my mentors who advised me to forget about my weaknesses, but instead to concentrate on my strengths. That was some of the best advice I ever received because prior to that, I had been focusing on improving my weaknesses so I could be a balanced person. I have come to learn that balance is overrated. Balanced people don't change the world, but people who focus on their strengths and purpose do—by God's grace.

Second Peter 1:8 says, "For if these things be in you, and abound, they make you that ye shall neither be barren nor unfruitful in the knowledge of our Lord Jesus Christ." I have meditated on that verse a great deal. It says that if we have and apply the knowledge, fruit is going to come. In the past, I listened to the voice of people who told me I could not do something—and I believed them. I must now become more receptive, sensitive, and obedient to the voice of God. Even when we don't know what we're doing or where we're going, He promised that He would lead and guide us. The Holy Spirit has been given to us to enlighten our minds and release the knowledge we need. That was why Peter wrote that we should not be barren or unfruitful in the knowledge of our Lord Jesus Christ.

My purpose journey will not end until the day I die and that is the reason I became more aware of my need to have the proper traveling companions. We need people around us who will feed our dreams and get excited with and for us. We need people who are also actively engaged in their own purpose quest so they can encourage us from their experience along the way. If we want to be fruitful, we need to be around people who are fruitful. We don't take advice about relationships from someone who's been married and divorced six times.

We have to learn to bend to superior knowledge. If someone has written 50 books, why should I argue with that person about what to put on my cover? I should take their advice until I am more experienced. I have watched Dr. Stanko's work evolve over the years. I read his book, *I Wrote This Book on Purpose . . . so You Can Know Yours*, and it changed my life. Then he wrote a devotional book on Proverbs.

I saw how easy he made it look. He writes a weekly column called *The Monday Memo* and makes writing so natural and easy. We saw how he did it because he was visible and willing to be transparent and accessible. We see how he writes something weekly and then turns what he writes into a book. Am I going to argue with him about how to do a book? No. We don't want to argue with people who know more than we do if we want those with experience who have been fruitful to be part of our lives

My grandmother used to say to me, "Birds of a feather flock together." That saying means that people can tell what kind of person they are looking at by knowing their friends and associates. She would button that up by saying, "Show me your friends and I will show you who you are." If we are around purpose-minded people, people who don't just talk but back up their talk with actions, it's going to cause us to be successful in our purpose. We will never feel God's approval or affirmation if we do not take a step of faith. People of action will teach us how to be action people as well.

Dr. Stanko said once that if we lift our feet up and there is nothing in front of us, if you are walking in faith, by the time we put our foot down, God will have created ground under that foot. I did not know what to do, whether to go forward or back to the ground behind me. Then I remembered that word he told me, and I have been moving forward ever since. Sometimes it's only little steps but who says we have to take huge steps? Therefore, I take little steps and become used to them so I can gain confidence to take bigger steps.

Dr. Stanko promised to share with us some relevant *Monday Memos* from his archive, so let me stop and give him the chance to fulfill his promise in the next two chapters.

CHAPTER TWELVE
THE MONDAY MEMO
JOHN W. STANKO

In my last chapter, I promised to share with you some of my *Monday Memos* that I have been producing every week since March of 2001. To date, I have published 920 of them, and they have included much of my insight into purpose, along with *Memos* on creativity, leadership, goal-setting, and faith. Here is the first *Memo* I ever wrote, and please notice where I was when I wrote it:

The Monday Memo

from the desk of Dr. John W. Stanko

Issue One

Hello and welcome to this first edition of the *Monday Memo*. My objective in writing is to help you focus this week on an issue that makes you more productive and fulfilled in your walk with the Lord. I am writing this week from Birmingham, England where I have been speaking on purpose and then conducting one-on-one interviews with people who are seeking to know who they are.

I have been reminded this past week of what Laurence Boldt wrote, which is also mentioned in my book, *I Wrote This Book on Purpose*:

> We make some attempt to answer them [the questions "who am I?" and "why am I here?"]. We ask our parents and teachers and it seems they do not know. They refer us to political and religious institutions, which often crank out canned answers devoid of personal meaning. Some even tell us that life has no meaning, save for eating and breeding. Most of us are smart enough to recognize that canned answers or begging the question will not do. We must find real answers for ourselves. But that takes more heart and effort than we are often willing to give.

How much are you willing to "give" this week to define who you are and who you are not. Can you spend 15 minutes a day? Can you ask those closest to you how they see you and what they think your strengths are? If you are willing to spend the time, prayerfully and diligently pursue the answers to these questions:

1. What situations seem to seek you out that you don't have to go looking for? Is there a problem that always finds its way to you to be solved? A certain type of person to which you find yourself drawn and effective? What kinds of jobs or ministries have given you the most joy?

2. What have people given you compliments about over the years that you don't think are very spiritual or special? Very often

those hold clues to your purpose.

3. Is there a passage of Scripture that is especially meaningful to you because it summarizes who you are and what you do best?

May I suggest a purpose journal where you can record the answers to these questions over time. I leave you with some verses from the book of Proverbs:

> My son [or daughter], if you accept my words and store up my commands within you, turning your ear to wisdom and applying your heart to understanding, and if you call out for insight and cry aloud for understanding, and if you look for it as for silver and search for it as for hidden treasure, then you will understand the fear of the Lord and find the knowledge of God (Proverbs 2:2-4).

Seek and keep on seeking your purpose. Don't give up and the Lord will reward you with clarity and direction.

******

Now here is *Memo* number 14:

The Monday Memo
from the desk of Dr. John Stanko
June 18, 2001: Issue Fourteen

I receive a lot of questions every week, and most of them focus on the issue of life purpose. Over the years, the questions asked most often, along with my answers, are as follows:

Q. Can my purpose change over time?

A. No. How you fulfill your purpose may change, but your purpose remains the same. I have fulfilled my purpose, which is to bring order out of chaos, in a number of different job roles. My purpose is the same; how I do it may change.

Q. Can I have more than one purpose?

A. No. You can have many gifts and talents, or different ways to express or fulfill your purpose, but your purpose is a clear, simple summary of your essence that is singular in focus.

Q. Should or can a husband and wife have the same purpose?

A. No. While it may be possible for a couple to have the same purpose, I have found it to be rare. Even if both work in the same business, mission, or ministry, each partner will have a different purpose, a different function in the same organization. Usually those purposes complement one another.

Q. What is the difference between a gift and purpose?

A. A gift is like a tool you carry with you to help fulfill your purpose. A plumber's purpose is not to "wrench." The wrench helps the plumber achieve his or her purpose to repair or build. Your gifts do the same for you, but they are not to be confused with your purpose.

Q. What is the difference between my ministry and my purpose?

A. I want to focus on this answer for the remainder of this *Monday Memo*. Too often we are tempted to separate what we do in church from what we do outside of church. We tend to think of ministry as related to church work, and purpose as something that may or may not fit into our church role. I contend that there is no difference between the two.

I met with a man in Atlanta, Georgia last year who has made a career in the field of human resources. Yet he was clearly a pastor. When I suggested that perhaps he was a chaplain or pastor in his company, he rejected the idea at first because he didn't have a pulpit or like public speaking. Yet he clearly had cared and "shepherd-ed" people for his entire corporate career. By the end of our meeting, he began to see his purpose was to care for people in a business setting. He began to see that his purpose *was* his ministry; it just wasn't taking place within the walls of a church building. That knowledge set him free to be who God made him to be and freed him from thinking that his ministry and purpose were two different things. They were not.

Perhaps you aren't clear about your purpose because you have put God in a box. You are a prophet, but everyone knows that prophets only function in a church setting. Who said that? You bring healing and wholeness to people, but don't lay hands on anyone or do it within a church. Does that limit your purpose or usefulness to God? Are you a preacher, but your pulpit is in a school or hospital? I met a man once whose title was school principal or headmaster but his purpose was to pastor the children who attended his school along with their parents.

As we close, read the words of Robert Greenleaf and be free to minister (which simply means to serve) in whatever setting the Lord chooses for you, whether it is in or outside the church:

> The great religious prophets of the future will not necessarily be theologians, philosophers, or people of literature. They are as likely to be lawyers, doctors, businesspeople, scientists, or politicians. And they will carry out their prophetic roles while functioning at a high level of excellence in their professional field. In fact, unless significant prophecy emerges in all of these places, the vision, without which the people perish, will not be sufficiently evident.
>
> The world society in which we are all inextricably involved is far too complex, it is in too revolutionary a mood, and it is fast becoming

too literate and aware of its sources of expertise for very much of the prophetic wisdom it needs to be uttered by ministers, scholars, or writers. These will, of course, continue to serve, but more on a par with those who are more immersed in the ongoing work of the world.

Businesses, government bureaus, law firms, clinics, and scientific laboratories have not only become large, sophisticated institutions and important sources of new knowledge, but they are just as likely to harbor a philosopher, a prophet, or a saint as is the monastery or the university. (source: *Seeker and Servant: Reflections on Religious Leadership*).

I hope this week you will find new peace to be who God made you to be in the setting that is best suited for you.

*****

Now here are two of my more popular *Monday Memos* that people have referred to again and again:

The Monday Memo
from the desk of Dr. John Stanko
Issue 19

I met with a man named Michael this week who has read my books. The church he attends was in part founded on the purpose message that he and others had read, and now he is employed there. But when I asked him what his purpose was, he said, "I'm not sure." So I did what I always do: I started asking questions.

It didn't take long for me to hear some key words: music, excellence, and projects were a few. But then one phrase jumped out at me. He said, "I like to make things sing." What a colorful phrase. He wasn't saying that everything had to be musical. "Making everything sing" stated his commitment to excellence in whatever he did. He didn't want things to "hum" or "whistle;" he wanted every project, whether musical or not, to be the best expression of their unique purpose. I left Michael to consider whether or not his life purpose is to make things sing.

I received many purpose inquiries this past week from people needing help finding their purpose. It occurred to me that I found my purpose—to bring order out of chaos—when I read those words in a book. Those words "jumped out" at me and I was never the same. I thought this week I would provide some phrases for you to study to see if the same thing would happen to you.

I found the list below in a book entitled, *Whistle While You Work: Heeding Your Life's Calling* by Richard Leider and David A. Shapiro. The authors refer to this as a list of "calling cards," a concept they developed to help people like you and me find our life's calling and purpose. They explain:

> Each of these callings describes a core gift. Each calling comes directly from someone's experience. We have been collecting callings in seminars, workshops, and coaching sessions with individuals and groups from all walks of life. The list of 52 callings we have come up with represent the "essence of essences" in our research. (This doesn't mean that there are not callings other than our 52; it does, however, mean that these 52 represent those that have best withstood real-world testing.) (San Francisco: Berrett-Koehler; 2001; page 35)

I am including half of their list this week and I will send the other half next week. Study both lists and see if anything stirs you. Feel free to focus on one of these phrases that seems a close description of who you are. Allow God to "energize" that statement and make it your own. Or modify it in some way to make it a better fit for you. I hope the Lord will do for you what He did for me. By taking someone else's words, I was able to define my purpose. Happy seeking.

List of Calling Cards

Category: Realistic

> 1) building things; 2) fixing things; 3) growing things; 4) making things work; 5) shaping environments; 6) solving problems

Category: Conventional

> 1) doing the numbers; 2) getting things right; 3) operating things; 4) organizing things; 5) processing things; 6) straightening things up

Category: Investigative

> 1) advancing ideas; 2) analyzing information; 3) investigating things; 4) getting to the heart of matters; 5) putting the pieces together; 6) researching things; 7) translating things; 8) discovering resources; 8) making connections

*****

The Monday Memo
from the desk of Dr. John Stanko
Issue 20

I suppose if I had lived in Alaska, my first book would have been titled, *Life is a Gold Mine: Can You Pan It?* as opposed to *Can You Dig It?* The early Alaskan settlers panned for gold in Alaska's streams and rivers in hopes of finding their treasure. With that in mind, I decided to try my hand at gold panning this past week while on an Alaskan cruise in a town called Skagway. More on where I panned later.

I did indeed find about 10 small pieces of gold

during my panning experience. And I found that if we are digging or panning for gold, it's certainly similar to what we go through to find our life purpose. How so? Consider these similarities:

1. **You can pan on your own, but having someone with you who knows how to do it is a great help**. My guide Tom began panning two years ago. He taught us the proper procedures that enabled each one of us to find gold. When you are looking for your purpose, it often helps to involve other people. Ask them what they think your purpose may be. Better yet, find someone who knows their purpose and ask them to help you find yours.

2. **Panning is hard work**. I stood over a trough for a few minutes panning for the gold I found and my back ached. I thought about those who panned in the cold Alaskan weather, standing in chilly water, and bending over for most of the day. Finding your purpose can be hard work, too; there is no guarantee when you'll find it or what you will have to go through to discover the big golden nugget called purpose.

3. **You don't need a lot of tools**. You only need a pan to pan for gold, not a lot of sophisticated equipment. That's how it is as you search for your purpose. You start where you are, with what you have, and look in faith.

4. **You can't see the gold right away**. When I began panning, my pan was filled with dirt and gravel. That's how it is when you search for your purpose; you can't see the "gold" because of all the other "stuff" in your life. It's there, however, and you simply have to know how to find it.

5. **It's exciting when you find the gold**. When I found the gold at the bottom of my pan, I felt like I was rich! When you find your life purpose, you feel the same way. The God of the universe knows who you are and gave you something to do that's just right for you.

6. **The gold stays in the pan**. Gold is so heavy that it's almost impossible to lose it when you're panning. Your life purpose is the same way; it's a part of you that goes with you wherever you are and is relevant no matter what mistakes you've made.

Last week I promised to give you the second half of the "calling cards" from the book entitled, *Whistle While You Work: Heeding Your Life's Calling* by Richard Leider and David A. Shapiro. If you just joined *The Monday Memo* family this week, the authors refer to the list below as calling cards, a concept they developed to help people like you and me find our life's calling and purpose. They explain:

> Each of these callings describes a core gift. Each calling comes directly from someone's experience. We have been collecting callings in seminars, workshops, and coaching sessions with individuals and groups from all walks of life. The list of 52 callings we have come up with represent the "essence of essences" in our research. (This doesn't mean that there are not callings other than our 52; it does, however mean that these 52 represent those that have best withstood real-world testing.) (San Francisco: Berrett-Koehler Publishers; page 35).

So are you ready to pan for gold? Put these calling cards in your pan and swirl them around to see if any stay in the bottom as the gold of your life. If you're not sure, then keep swirling them around in your mind and heart. Keep looking and I promise that you'll find the riches that lie in all the "stuff" in your life. I hope it all pans out!

Category: Enterprising

> 1) bringing out potential; 2) empowering others; 3) exploring the way; 4) making deals;

5) managing things; 6) opening doors; 7) persuading people; 8) selling intangibles; 9) starting things

Category: Social

1) awakening spirit; 2) bringing joy; 3) building relationships; 4) creating dialogue; 5) creating trust; 6) facilitating change; 7) getting participation; 8) giving care; 9) healing wounds; 10) helping overcome obstacles; 11) instructing people; 12) resolving disputes

Category: Artistic

1) adding humor; 2) breaking molds; 3) creating things; 4) composing things; 5) designing things; 6) moving through space; 7) performing events; 8) seeing possibilities; 9) seeing the big picture; 10) writing things

✶✶✶✶✶

I have to confess that I thoroughly enjoyed going back through the first 20 *Memos* I wrote, and I included more of them in this chapter than I anticipated because they are still good teaching tools. I can see why the *Memo* has lasted for as long as it has. It was regular (people could count on it showing up) and it has had good content.

Pastor Yvonne mentioned the concept of fruit and God's desire that we produce it. Let's look at a few more Memos that focus on that topic as I conclude what I have to contribute in *Connected: Colleagues on Purpose.*

CHAPTER THIRTEEN

FRUIT AND THE FUNNEL EFFECT

JOHN W. STANKO

After I taught on the concept of purpose for a few years, I had someone advise me that I needed to broaden my repertoire of messages. He felt I was getting too narrow in my thinking and, if I was going to be a successful teacher or consultant, I needed more. I considered this man's advice and felt like I did have more already. I had written and taught about what I called the five Gold Mine Principles of purpose, creativity, goals, time management, and faith. I also taught about such topics as leadership in general (servant leadership in particular), our mind as the source of personal transformation, and all sorts of Bible study topics (leadership, Proverbs, and the Psalms, just to name a few).

While I considered this man's advice, I rejected it and instead decided to dig down even deeper into the concept of purpose. I determined that I was going to be one of the best purpose coaches and authors in the world by devoting myself to study, counseling, coaching, and writing. I found that this focus did not limit me, but rather opened the entire world to me of those who could benefit from my purpose of creating order out of chaos.

I have found that some people are hesitant where purpose is concerned because they believe it is too restrictive and will limit what they can do, thus making them useful in only certain situations. I have found the opposite to be true and I wrote about it in a *Monday Memo*, which I include a portion of here:

The Funnel Effect

A funnel is wide at the top and very narrow at the bottom so that liquids may be poured into something with a small opening. When you begin your PurposeQuest, you are at the top of the funnel. The whole world and all its options are available to you. Then something happens that can unnerve you and make you uncomfortable. As you progress down the funnel of purpose, you may begin to feel restricted in your activity. Things you once did have no meaning or you lose your enthusiasm for things you once had energy to do. You also may find that you evaluate everything you do differently. As you go down the funnel, you find there is no room or time to do some of those things that are no longer related to your purpose.

Some are concerned that their lives will be less meaningful if they get to the bottom of the funnel. They can't see how God can use them when they seem to be doing so little. To the contrary, the bottom of the funnel is your point of greatest effectiveness. It is at that point where you find what you do that no one else can do. While it seems restrictive, that point allows God to send you anywhere in the world that needs who you are and what you do. The narrow point is why the funnel exists; without it, there would be no purpose for the larger, top portion of the funnel.

God is narrowing my activity so I can be more effective with greater impact. My pruning that is restricting my activities is actually making me more focused. This year (2018) I should finish and publish six books while helping 25 others publish theirs by serving as their creative consultant and editor. I am doing more media, mostly video, and I am also speaking more on leadership issues, while I consult and coach for those who want to be better leaders.

What are you holding on to that is restricting the funnel effect in your own life? Is your fear that you won't have any money causing you to hold on to some activities that have lost their life and interest for you? I urge you to follow my lead and embark on a self-pruning journey. Allow God to take you to new places that will lead to new fruitfulness as you let go of things that are important and dear but cannot make the trip down your funnel with you as seek your point of maximum potential and usefulness.

I mention an important word you should remember in the excerpt above, and that word is *pruning*. When God prunes us, we often feel like we have done something wrong and have missed Him in some way. To the contrary, God prunes us when we are fruitful and His goal is to make us even more fruitful, as Jesus explained:

> "I am the true vine, and my Father is the gardener. He cuts off every branch in me that bears no fruit, while every branch that does bear fruit he prunes so that it will be even more fruitful. You are already clean because

of the word I have spoken to you. Remain in me, as I also remain in you. No branch can bear fruit by itself; it must remain in the vine. Neither can you bear fruit unless you remain in me.

"I am the vine; you are the branches. If you remain in me and I in you, you will bear much fruit; apart from me you can do nothing. If you do not remain in me, you are like a branch that is thrown away and withers; such branches are picked up, thrown into the fire and burned. If you remain in me and my words remain in you, ask whatever you wish, and it will be done for you. This is to my Father's glory, that you bear much fruit, showing yourselves to be my disciples" (John 15:1-8).

Our relationship with the Lord is not about going to church and behaving ourselves—although both are important practices. Our relationship with Him is to bear fruit, and that is why purpose and creativity are so important, along with understanding our personality and how we will approach our work and other people.

This leads me to a question I want to pose: What is your fruit? Can you describe it? Jesus warned in Matthew 21:43: "Therefore I tell you that the kingdom of God will be taken away from you and given to a people who will produce its fruit." Let me go to another *Monday Memo* to discuss this concept of fruit.

*****

Monday Memo: The Fruit Process

I reflected this past week on what it takes for actual, edible fruit to be produced. Here are some thoughts on the matter:

1. Fruit is fragile and conditions must be

right for it to come forth—climate, soil, free from frost, not too much rain (or too little). The same is true for spiritual fruit.

2. Fruit starts with a blossom, which is pretty and fragrant, but is only the beginning. There are many believers who blossom and have great potential to bear fruit, but that potential must be nurtured.

3. If fruit is eaten before it is ripe, it can be toxic (or make someone sick). The same is true for spiritual fruit. It requires maturity for it to taste the best.

4. Fruit is meant for two things: to be consumed by others or to produce seed so that more fruit can be produced. All spiritual fruit is for the benefit of other people to consume as they need it.

5. Fruit usually has a short lifespan and must be consumed quickly or it will rot and go to waste. No one knows how many days they have to bear fruit, so it must be produced and distributed with a sense of urgency.

6. Fruit requires an ongoing process of pruning and fertilizing its source, or bad or paltry fruit will be produced. Believers must continue to nurture themselves spiritually if they are to continue to bear more and better fruit.

The Research Is In and . . .

I spent some time reading what others have written about fruit and one thing is for certain: Most people have described what fruit is like (just as I did above) but they are hesitant to come out and say what we should be looking for in our lives that can be called fruit. Some do say that it is souls saved or people we lead to the Lord. Yet, if truth be told, most people do not lead many people to the Lord. Others say it is a vibrant prayer life, but is fruit defined as the number of prayers a believer says in his or her lifetime? Finally, some identify fruit as correct doctrine, but that makes fruit an intellectual pursuit.

Therefore, below I offer my definition of Kingdom fruit, and challenge you to identify what this fruit is in your life. Once you identify it (or if you already know what it is), then I challenge you to determine how you can be even more fruitful. But first, here is my definition:

> *following your joy as you combine your God-given gifts, creativity, purpose, experience, interests, and sustained effort in a way that produces something of value for the benefit of others and yourself.*

My fruit is comprised of the books I have written; the libraries I have helped establish in Kenya; the classes I have taught at university; the devotionals I have written, published, and posted on social media for 16 years; and the seminars I have conducted on purpose and creativity. Oh yes, and as the Spirit has produced His fruit in my life, it has translated into tangible expressions of empathy for others in painful and difficult situations to which I formerly paid little attention.

Let me close with this thought: All fruit is measurable and measured. We speak of fruit as a cluster, a bunch, peck, half-bushel, bushel, pound, kilo, acre, or hectare. Therefore, I assume that your fruit, even though it's spiritual, must be measurable as well. Spend some time praying and thinking about the question, "What is my fruit?" and then follow the answer up with another: "How can I produce more of it?" If you persevere in seeking the answers, you will bear the fruit of the Kingdom in your life that God expects and enjoys. Don't be afraid of the funnel effect either, for it is God's way of narrowing your focus so you can maximize your effectiveness in the time you have left on Earth.

*****

There you have my contribution to this collaboration called *Connected: Colleagues on Purpose.* I didn't mention that this book is the result of a word the Lord spoke to me in 2018. I was driving along listening to music and realized how many duets I have in my iTunes library, mostly of a man and a woman singing. The Lord whispered to me "sing duets" and I knew right away that I was to produce some books with female partners. Shortly thereafter, Pastor Yvonne contacted me to write for her Women of Purpose twentieth anniversary and I asked her, "Do you want to write a book with me?" True to her High-I personality, she said yes right away. This book is the fulfillment of that directive and idea.

I hope you have enjoyed this effort and I trust there will be others that come forth from our relationship. From here, I will let Pastor Yvonne wrap up and we also have some testimonies from women who have been impacted by the purpose message to close out this book. My contact information will be at the end of the book, and I hope you will write me to share your purpose story or ask your purpose question. I never tire of talking about purpose, so you won't bother me at all if you write. In fact, you will help me fulfill my purpose of creating order out of chaos. Thank you and may God bless your quest for purpose as you connect with Him and other purpose seekers.

CHAPTER FOURTEEN
LESSONS LEARNED
YVONNE E. BROOKS

In this last chapter, I want to share with you some things I have learned while conducting women's ministry for almost twenty years. Many people have come to me requesting, pleading with me, to do this, that, or the other—like an event, a program, or a book. Those are the same people who do not turn up after you take their advice and do those things. People love to share their creativity with me so they don't have to do it or partner with it, and that has been discouraging at times. Yet, that has taught me to keep my ear to the ground and listen to God.

I have also learned from experience to trust my judgment, to look at a cat, recognize it as such, and not allow someone else to talk me into thinking it's not a cat. That means I have had to learn to trust my judgment and the work God has done in my life. I have allowed people to talk me out of what I knew because I assumed they knew better than I—particularly when it came to my own abilities. Now I listen to God and His leading *before* I follow anyone else's. I have also learned to trust what's in my heart because He is the Lord of my heart

I have heard women say all kinds of spiritual things and make commitments, but often the thing they really want is to get married. Why is that? It's because they don't have a good sense of self-esteem and think they need a man to complete them. How many of those same women end up divorced? In my experience, many do. They had a flawed idea about marriage and what it would do for them before they entered into the marriage covenant.

I would love to see women believe in themselves and see themselves as having worth and value—apart from marriage. What I have noticed over the years is that women who have that sense of confidence and who are pursuing something on their own are the ones men are attracted to—and those are the ones who are happily married.

Another thing I noticed is how male-dominated our churches tend to be. I'm not a women's libber by any means and I'm not saying the church should go to extremes to correct a problem from the past. Even if women are elevated to a position they have never had before, it is the men's voices that tend to be heard. Men have the last word, which is why men are going to have to play a role in releasing the women.

I'm not content for us to go through the motions of ministering to women to have them feel better. I want them to be released to fulfill their purpose, both in and out of the church. If the belief in a woman's role is not really changing, we're just going through the motions. At the end of the day, God wants us to love Him and one another. How do we love one another when some see the need for women to be under someone's thumb? That mentality has changed some, but it's still prevalent. Women are often not seen as equals. The Scripture says that we are neither male nor female, but we are one in Christ Jesus. That is the kind of equality I'm talking about, but this may be too radical for some.

I have heard the comments that show how many lives have been changed through Dr. Stanko's writings and many of them are from women. That's because women can sense he is really invested in them finding their purpose. He does not have a hidden agenda or an ulterior motive. At the end of the day, I don't want to be a bishop because I don't want that kind of responsibility. I don't want to have to make laws and rules. I am quite happy to be led, but I am concerned about the manner by which I am led. Even though we may have one or two outstanding men who understand this issue, I find the majority of the men are still misogynistic.

I heard Dr. Stanko talk years ago about the servant's heart. I have actively cultivated a spirit of servanthood instead of a spirit of entitlement. I don't want to receive honor or anything else simply because I have the title of pastor. There should be no standard that says I am to be treated with special honor. That is something I don't want anywhere in my thinking. I'm here to serve. Can you imagine if I serve the people and the people served me in whatever way they saw fit? Can you imagine how the church would be? It would be totally amazing. They call me First Lady, and want me to have an armourbearer. I don't want all that.

I'm in the process of encouraging our young people to look at what they want to do, whether it's to be an actor, a model, or whatever. I tell them to pursue it and assure them I'm praying for them because God needs them out there to be salt and light. What if we put the salt in the safe, locked it up, and threw away the key? How does that benefit anyone? We have to release people into their purpose and let God use them the way He planned.

We should not tell them, "You can't do that." We need to help and equip them. Whenever young people came to me and said, "I want to go to university or here or there," I was afraid I was losing control of them, and I had to deal with that in my heart. *Who are they supposed to obey, God or you?* I had to learn to let go and encourage them to go for it. I encourage them to listen for their purpose and listen to God's voice; then do what He says. I had to teach myself that they are not here to please me. They are here to please God, but the problem was that we were pressured to please men or to gain the approval of the pastor.

Lately, Dr. Stanko has been emphasizing the negative role fear has played in our lives as we seek purpose or express creativity. I have certainly had to battle my fears, and it is never-ending warfare. We don't ever get over fear after one battle, for the battle is a way of life. The enemy of our soul knows what our weaknesses are, and he will keep pointing them out, accusing us of being flawed. We have to become experts at overcoming fear whenever it appears, and it is always manifesting. That is why we must have courage and faith. If we did not have any adversaries or obstacles to overcome, why would we need faith?

We cannot gauge the impact of what we are doing because it's hard to see ourselves as others see us. I was talking to a guest minister at our church and that guest said to me, "Pastor Yvonne, you sang and it opened the atmosphere for God to work and move." I did not know or see that. That is the reason it is important to have mentors who will speak honestly into our lives. We think we need them to tell us the negative things about us, and that may be true, but we need them to help us see what we do well and then overcome the false humility that prevents us from acknowledging, "Yes, this is who God made me to be and when I express it, I glorify Him." Then we need to do the same for others, speaking honestly and without fear that it will be taken the wrong way or that people will become proud. We are not to inflate our importance but we are to accept that we *are* important to what God is doing

I have always been troubled with fear, as I mentioned earlier, and I have learned it is part of my High-I personality for we are afraid of being rejected. The fear would paralyze me and keep me from doing what I should be doing. While working as a mental health nurse, I would counsel people who felt fear to do something anyway. I finally started to take my own advice. Sometimes I did fail, but I found I learned so much from my failures that it became an advantage. My attitude now is even if I am afraid, I take my confidence in both hands and press forward. If we don't do that, nothing will get done. Courage is not an absence of fear, but learning how to function in the midst of fear.

I mentioned my trips to Zimbabwe and South Africa and did you notice that I did not go alone. I took people with me because I know I need a team. What I do, I can do very well by God's Spirit, but I am limited in what I can do. That is the reason I have to take people with me and work in teams, instead of working alone. I am learning to delegate authority along with the responsibility by giving people meaningful work and getting out of the way so they can get things done. When I took the ladies with me to Africa, I exposed them to my world, work, and friends and it changed their lives. I have learned to work toward the outcomes rather than obsessing over the details. I am allowing others to exercise their creativity, and as long as we get the results, I am happy.

I have learned to lean on the support from my family, those who are nearest and dearest to me. When I take them with me, not necessarily on the road, but into purpose, it is quite affirming and rewarding. We are all learning not to light a light and then put a bushel over it. We must all shine with the light of purpose and be who God made us to be. I am so glad my children and now my grandchildren have learned that much earlier in life than I did.

As we close, when you seek and find purpose, at first you will feel like you are wearing shoes too big for you. My advice is to continue and stay true to what you know, for in time the shoes will begin to fit perfectly. You have a purpose and when you express it, you are part-nering with God. God values you as an individual and is faithful to give you the skills to carry out purpose. Believe me, it is a mountain-top experience when you do. My life has been enhanced and increased in value because of purpose. People I've never met come up to me to thank me for doing what I have done. All I did was obey what God birthed me to do to be a door opener for others.

Speaking of others thanking me, I want to close this book by sharing the stories from the Women of Purpose twentieth anniversary from women who have become near and dear to me. They are among the fruit of my purpose journey and my story of *Connected* would not be complete without hearing from them. At the end of the book, you will find information on how to reach me if the need arises. You won't have to look hard or far, for I know my purpose star is rising and it won't be hard to find if you look. Thank you and God bless you.

EPILOGUE

Happy 21st anniversary and huge congratulations to 'Women of Purpose' and its visionary, Pastor Yvonne Brooks! It's hard to comprehend that this conference has been running for 21 years, particularly when I recall being at the very first one way back in 1998. How time has flown!

I made the decision to attend the first conference, then known as Women In the Word, because my mind was in turmoil, having conflicting thoughts about my purpose. Buried somewhere deep down inside of me, I had a feeling God wanted to use me in ministry, but I was at a place where I felt my failures in life had disqualified me from such a privilege. In my mind, I felt worthless to God, as I had tied my value to the numerous mistakes I had made and also to the disappointments of the past.

I attended the conference not quite sure what to expect, but knowing I could not continue in the mode I was in. I recall the first session, which I believe we called 'The Trashing Session', where we acknowledged everything we needed to get rid of, wrote them down, binned them, and they were then burnt. That action of confessing and repenting before God gave me a freedom I had not experienced in years. Not only did I bin sin, I also binned self-doubt, low self-esteem, restrictive thoughts, and hindrances to my own progress. I was free!

As God spoke over the three days, I realised His Kingdom had come and I was an integral part of His plan. I had work to do but God had not changed His mind about the part He purposed for me to play in His Kingdom. I left with a renewed zeal, vigour, and focus to take my rightful place. I attended the conference for several years after that time and each year I received strategies that helped to equip me fulfil the call of God on my life. One of my greatest pleasures was the time spent sitting or lying silently in God's presence, being able to hear Him clearly giving me directions for my life. It was surreal!

In March 2003, I was appointed as a local minister in my home church, Faith Chapel. Since that time, I have taught and preached not only in the local assembly and organisation, but in various churches and organisations in the U.K., in Europe, the United States, and Jamaica. In the last few years, God has led me to minister to wounded and broken women, helping them allow God into those wounded areas so He can heal, liberate, and use them for His glory. Five years ago, I qualified to become a licensed minister with the Pentecostal Assemblies of the World, Inc., and was just recently consecrated in this area. To

God be the glory!

The Women of Purpose Conference helped me see that God was fully acquainted with all my faults and failures before I ever experienced them, yet He still chose and anointed me to set the captives free. Thank you, God bless you, and happy anniversary Women of Purpose! – *Evangelist Laurice Murphy, Faith Chapel, Pentecostal Assemblies of the World, Inc.*

*****

Women of Purpose Ambassador

Twenty-one years ago, I attended my first women's conference. It was a Sunday evening when I saw the flyer headed Women In the Word on the church noticeboard and without hesitation, I knew I was going. I mentioned it to a couple of the sisters who said they too wanted to attend. Before we knew it, there were a couple of car loads of ladies on the way to the country. I never had a clue or vague imagination I would find myself in Shropshire. I remember thinking I was driving to a farm.

Yes, my desire to go caused me to be the driver of my late aunt's (Evangelist June Cranston) very large Citroen through the countryside. The venue was basic. There was no TV and from my recollection, no mobile phone service. It was clear from the off that this was the place to meet with God without distractions; we were cut off from the outside world. From the offset of the meeting, the presence of God was evident; there was no uncertainty that this was God ordained. The atmosphere was such that if we wanted to be rescued from our burdens, we had come to the right place.

This first conference was pivotal in my life because I was facing my own personal battles and challenges. During this period, I was burdened, sad, and hurting and I guess somewhat disappointed in myself. As a seasoned church attendee, I knew how to internalise the anguish of an unhappy marriage, one that had been so since the honeymoon.

It may have been on the second day that a shift took place in my broken spirit. I was able to pour my heart out to God, crying and sobbing uncontrollably. Prayer General and Intercessor Evangelist Linda Daniels from Mount Calvary ministered to me through the power of the Holy Spirit. She was comforting and reassuring as she spoke words of healing. I remember such a release coming over me; there was healing in my tears and her words. Even when the session was over, the outpouring of the Holy Spirit was evident in many of the sisters. The following day my deliverance was realised when, I think it may have been the last session of the meeting, I was able to burst out with great thanks and appreciation to my Father. It was so complete having the Holy Spirit wash over me afresh.

All of the ladies who attended from Faith Chapel went on to another level; it was so evident that we had been with God. The anointing of the Holy Spirit was plain to see as soon as we walked into the church service on the Sunday following. From then on I became an ardent support of what became Women of Purpose and have attended the conference for most years. I would often encourage women to attend this life-changing conference; it was so that I heard somebody describe it as "Dahlia's conference." I'm glad to be associated with such an anointed ministry where I have witnessed the lives of many women transform. Over the years a few of the *early* speakers that spring to mind are:

- Sister Caroline Malcolm: She spoke about Lazarus, using a demonstration of someone wrapped in bandages.
- Sister Sherri Smith (now Brogdan): intercessor

- Sister Linda Daniels: intercessor
- Bishop Clifton Jones: Prayer Clinic General
- Elder Jerome Jones
- Clive Pick: Kingdom Economics and Tithing
- Sister Donna Napolitan: Operating in the prophetic
- Pastor Winnie McCleod: Deliverance Ministry
- John Stanko: Purpose specialist

Congratulations to Pastor Yvonne Brooks who has poured into my life over the years. May God continue to bless you in His abundance. Thank you for the sacrifices you have made over the years. You are truly a blessing. – *Dahlia Rose*

*****

Pioneering New Territory

Over twenty-one years ago, there was a groaning in the realm of the Spirit for a progressive women's movement that would empower and equip women for ministry. Pastor Yvonne pioneered such a movement, a movement that went beyond denominational and cultural boundaries to bring together the body of Christ. It was new, exciting, and fresh. Women were called from a place of obscurity into a place of service in the kingdom of God. Initially we would meet for prayer and Bible study in my home or Pastor Yvonne's home.

As we began to meet and pray, Pastor Yvonne felt the need for a retreat to broaden the ministry so we could embrace other women. A vision was birthed and Pastor Yvonne felt it was imperative to move with the word of God. The vision of the Lord is always bigger than our capabilities or our resources. It can be overwhelming indeed and may cause us to run away or even faint. It is imperative to hear the Lord and trust in His leading. We did not know how God was going to do it or if the women were going to embrace the concept of women gathering from different denominations. As part of the team, we agreed with the vision the Lord had given to Pastor Yvonne. A voice can propel the vision forward, delay it, or even cause us to abort the vision.

At that time, I was Pastor Yvonne's armourbearer. The newly-birthed ministry did not have any financial resources, so I gave Pastor Yvonne the deposit for the first Women of Purpose retreat. I learned over time that I had to align myself with others who were walking out their Kingdom mandate. It was imperative that I served in whatever capacity I could. I did not know the Lord was setting me up to glean from the Brooks' field, for later I too became a pastor.

I soon realized that declaring and fighting for a vision the Lord has given us are never easy tasks. The vision is transposed from heaven into our hearts, and our minds will tend to defy all logic and reason; our resources, means, skills, and surroundings are not usually conducive to the vision. It will often cause our minds to ponder how it will come to pass. Vision can be exciting and scary at the same time, and it can become contradictory as we occupy both ends of the spectrum simultaneously—the desire for change but the fear of changing.

In the process of developing a vision, we will sometimes hit roadblocks, setbacks, or even experience the death of the vision. Pastor Yvonne never let anything hinder the work of the Lord. She realized that the vision of the Lord was given to forge a process of change in the lives of the women, their ministries, and the community.

Women of Purpose has changed many lives over the years, including mine. The journey over twenty-one years has been amazing—from meeting in my home to attending retreat centers and now hotels. We have come a long way. I remember we used to go ahead of time to the retreat center and decorate the pulpit area and rooms, and also to fast and pray. It was amazing to see great deliverance among the women. The transformation was evident, as women would leave revived and refreshed with renew hope and a clear vision for their lives and ministry.

I salute and honor Pastor Yvonne for the great work she has done and continues to do. She has been an inspiration and a role model to many. Thank you for pioneering new territory; you have set a standard all women in ministry should aspire to achieve. I love you, my dear sister, and friend. I look forward to the great things God has in store for this ministry. - *Dr. Claudette Morgan-Scott*

*****

Congratulations to my friend, Pastor Yvonne Brooks, on the twentieth anniversary of her ministry, Women of Purpose. I consider it an honor to have played a role in the start of this important organization. It is a source of joy to look back over the last twenty years and see how God has used Women of Purpose and Pastor Brooks, and to reflect on my own purpose journey during that time. Pastor Yvonne asked me to reminisce a bit about the last two decades, and I hope my memory serves me correctly as I write. If not, just consider that my brain is has a lot more memories to recall than it had in 2001.

After I founded my ministry named PurposeQuest in 2000, Yvonne Brooks was one of the first people I met, having been introduced by Bishop Keith McLeod. After Pastor Brooks sat for a personality profile and heard the purpose message, she said, "You *must* come to our church and make this presentation." I had experienced many people who made such a declaration, but most never followed through. That wasn't the case with Pastor Brooks. She got in touch with me right away and I came to Birmingham in March of 2001.

After that first visit, Pastor Yvonne informed me that she was renaming her organization called Women In the Word to Women of Purpose. If I remember correctly, I came to three or four of the first purpose conferences and God was always present in a special way. One year, I brought with me some of my students from the university where I teach and they still talk about the experience they had with both the ladies at the conference and also the presence of the Lord.

During the conferences, many of the ladies would complete a personality profile and then I would have a one-on-one meeting with them to talk about who they were and who they were not. That would invariably lead to a discussion of purpose and many women came face-to-face, some for the first time, with the fact that God has assigned them a purpose, wanted them to know what it was, and would then help them fulfill it. I still maintain contact with some of those ladies through Facebook and I have published a book for one woman I met at a conference.

When I think of how I have changed and grown since 2001, it takes my breath away. God has been faithful to help me spread the good news of purpose in many ways. I have 1) written 920 weekly *Monday Memos*; 2) published 45 books, many of which touch or focus on purpose; 3) spent extensive time in Africa to profile individuals, build teams, and talk purpose; 4) started a nonprofit organization, PurposeQuest International, that has done relief work in Africa and also spread the purpose message; 5) started Urban Press, a publishing company to help others broadcast their purpose stories; 6) finished a verse-by-verse commentary on the entire New Testament; and 7) helped twelve people found their own nonprofit organizations as a means to fulfill their purpose.

I have served the purpose message my entire adult life and there is no end in sight, although I know my days ahead of me are less than those behind me. That only inspires me to do all I can do to help as many people as possible hear about and find purpose. I still meet regularly with people to coach them around purpose issues, using the personality profiles to get people talking about who they are—and who they are not. To help me coach, I have a set of questions I ask to help people think about purpose. As I close, I leave you with those questions and suggest you pick one or two and seek the Lord for answers so you can be clear about your purpose.

1. For what have people complimented you on a regular basis?

2. What gives you joy and excites your will?

3. How would you spend your time if money to live on wasn't an issue?

4. What did you find yourself daydreaming about when you were child, or even as an adult?

5. What makes you angry? What makes you cry?

6. What do you do that when you do it, you lose track of time and forget to eat?

7. Is there a Bible verse or passage that best explains who you are or what you do best?

8. What are you afraid of that is keeping you from embracing your purpose?

9. Has a godly person spoken anything to you that described who you are or what you would do?

10. If you lost your job tomorrow and had a six-month severance package, what would you do during those six months?

I have many more resources on my website to help you find purpose, including a purpose assessment that will give you a score to let you know where I think you are in your PurposeQuest. Come visit me at www.purposequest.com and let me know if I can help you in any way as you seek purpose. (My email is johnstanko@gmail.com and I am on Facebook and Twitter @johnstanko.) Thank you and may the Lord allow Himself to be found as you seek Him with all your heart. – *Dr. John Stanko, PurposeQuest International*

✶✶✶✶✶

When I received the request to share some of my experiences about Women of Purpose, I considered it a privilege. As I began to reflect, I realized I have far too many fond memories to share in one writing. I was first invited by Pastor Yvonne Brooks to be a guest for one of the Women of Purpose retreats to share my ministry of dance. Although that was a major part of the ministry God had given me to share throughout the United States, it was an honor to have the opportunity to share my gift in England. From my very first visit, I was warmly welcomed and received. Within moments, it was apparent I was ordained by God to be there. Soon after, as the Lord would have it in His infinite wisdom, I was invited to share as a guest speaker. As each speaker came, although we were all different in our presentation and delivery, the Spirit of the Lord was our unique bond, and we were united with a common goal. It was the uninhibited, unprecedented power of the God's anointing that was released in every venue where we assembled.

During the years when I was a part of Women of Purpose, I can say I matured spiritually by leaps and bounds. I learned so much through my spiritual encounters and freedom in worship that I had not experienced before. It was clear that the women who assembled for this annual conclave were single in mind and purpose. With that level of anticipation and in that unusually charged atmosphere, God was given free rein to do anything—and that He did!

My life has been tremendously and positively impacted by the long-lasting relationships that have stood the test of time and distance that separates us. I give honor to and salute the visionary and founder, Pastor Yvonne Brooks, for her leadership and passion for women of all nations to achieve their destiny. I personally was a recipient of her passion from the start of our relationship, and as a result, my eyes were opened to so much more that God had in store for my future and what God had predestined for my life.

My prayer is that God's hand of favor will continue to rest upon Pastor Yvonne Brooks and all those who share the execution of this great assignment. May every woman who passes through the portals of Women of Purpose be as blessed as I have been. My love for you all continues. – *Pastor Denise B. Carpenter, God's Way Ministries International, Columbus, Ohio*

✶✶✶✶✶

Greetings to all the women of our great God and congratulations on this twenty-first year of ministry. Being a member from the birthing of Women In the Word way back in 1997 with the words from Pastor Yvonne Brooks, the visionary of this women's ministry: "The women need to go higher in God, in the Word, and in prayer." Then I remember meeting at Claudette Daley's home in Wolverhampton with Avril, Jean Anderson, and Elaine Davies for prayer and planning of the first conference. The late nights and the early get ups are not to be forgotten. The focal point was integrity and purity.

I remember arriving at Cloverley Hall Christian Conference Centre in Whitchurch ready for a great move of God. Preparations were in full flow as we awaited the arrival of our local and international guests. We worked to ensure the sanctuary, welcome packs, bedrooms, and tape ministry were ready. My two most memorable recognitions, were the Ministry of Dance by Sister Alison O'Conner who took us to a place of worship like never before and the last morning of the conference, when all were in the sanctuary. The atmosphere was full of God's presence, the worship and anointing were overflowing, and many ladies were slain in the Spirit as Evangelist Donna Napolitan ministered in the prophetic ministry with a blow, like a mighty rushing wind came upon all who came forward for prayer, only to see the rows of ladies out cold under the anointing.

Whilst this was in operation, the bell kept ringing from the food hall as lunch was ready, but the sanctuary was 'sealed by the Holy Spirit' and no one wanted to leave the room. There was an awesome anointing and presence of God. There was an urgency and hunger for God to fill us up. We had a time of Intimacy with God our Father, our Beloved and an open forum for genuine fellowship and for one's ministry to be birthed. May God's best be yours moving forward from Women In The Word, continuing as Women of Purpose. – *Lorna Jones, Mount Peniel Church, Stafford*

*****

Shortly after I was baptized, my sister invited me to join her at a women's retreat. I was hesitant to go since I was new in the faith and not sure I was ready for such an intense and personal time with other believers. Little did I know how that time would change my life! It was there that I had my personality profile done which began a journey of self-awareness that has yet to stop. That journey has led me to leadership roles and possibilities

I never imagined were possible. My congratulations to Pastor Yvonne Brooks for the twentieth anniversary of Women of Purpose. I know my life is not the only one that was radically changed by our time at WOP, and I pray many others will continue to benefit from the commitment to purpose and excellence that are trademarks of Pastor Yvonne's work. God bless you all! - *Felicia Linch, owner and director of Kitch Consulting and Coaching Ltd., operating throughout the Caribbean*

PASTOR YVONNE E. BROOKS

Yvonne Elizabeth Brooks is the first assistant pastor of New Jerusalem Apostolic Church—a thriving church that is having a huge impact in the community in the city of Birmingham. She is a qualified Behavioural Consultant, Mental Health Nurse and Registered General Nurse and from this, she has a passion for seeing people receive deliverance, healing, and restoration.

Pastor Yvonne has completed a Bachelor's Degree in Biblical Studies and a Doctorate in Theology and Biblical Studies as testament to her desire to grow and develop so she can be a blessing to others as she delivers the Word nationally and internationally. She has also presented on television and radio and is the author of two books: *Touching God's Heart: Prayers that Make a Difference* and *Purpose Steps*. As a result of her ongoing service, she has been recognised with a number of awards including the Women of Excellence Trailblazer Award.

Her main achievement is being the founder and director of Women of Purpose Ministries, which inspires women around the globe to become women of purpose so they can take their place on the world stage. WOP is a ministry that encompasses a number of life-changing programmes, including the Women of Purpose Conference, Esther's International Program, Esther's Extra, NEXT Steps, EXCEL, Ambassador, and Tohorah (a retreat for teenagers). Her desire is to help others to transform life's broken places to a place of life-long fulfilment and purpose. (To learn more, please visit her website at http://www.esthersacademy.co.uk).

The greatest achievement of her life is her beautiful family, which has stemmed from over four decades of marriage to Bishop M.A. Brooks. Together they have three talented children and two grandchildren, Jade and Zion.

PASTOR JOHN W. STANKO

John Stanko was born in Pittsburgh, Pennsylvania. After graduating from St. Basil's Prep School in Stamford, Connecticut, he attended Duquesne University where he received his bachelor's and master's degrees in economics in 1972 and 1974 respectively.

Since then, John has served as an administrator, teacher, consultant, author, and pastor in his profession-al career. He holds a second master's degree in pastoral ministries, and earned his doctorate in pastoral ministries from Liberty Theological Seminary in Houston, Texas in 1995. He recently completed a second doctor of ministry degree at Reformed Presbyterian Theological Seminary in Pittsburgh.

John has taught extensively on the topics of time management, life purpose and organization, and has conducted leadership and purpose training sessions throughout the United States and in 32 countries. He is also certified to administer the DISC and other related personality assessments as well as the Natural Church Development profile for churches. In 2006, he earned the privilege to facilitate for The Pacific Institute of Seattle, a leadership and personal development program, and for

The Leadership Circle, a provider of cultural and executive 360-degree profiles. He has authored fifteen books and written for many publications around the world.

John founded a personal and leadership development company, called PurposeQuest, in 2001 and today travels the world to speak, consult and inspire leaders and people everywhere. From 2001-2008, he spent six months a year in Africa and still enjoys visiting and working on that continent, while teaching for Geneva College's Masters of Organizational Leadership and the Center for Urban Biblical Ministry in his hometown of Pittsburgh, Pennsylvania. John has been married for 44 years to Kathryn Scimone Stanko, and they have two adult children and two grandchildren. In 2009, John was appointed the administrative pastor for discipleship at Allegheny Center Alliance Church on the North Side of Pittsburgh where he served for five years. Most recently, John founded Urban Press, a publishing service designed to tell stories of the city, from the city, and to the city.

Keep in Touch with John W. Stanko

www.purposequest.com
www.johnstanko.us
www.stankobiblestudy.com
www.stankomondaymemo.com
or via email at johnstanko@gmail.com

John also does extensive relief and community development work in Kenya. You can see some of his projects at www.purposequest.com/contributions

PurposeQuest International
PO Box 8882
Pittsburgh, PA 15221-0882